JEWS BY CHOICE
A Study of Converts to Reform and Conservative Judaism

JEWS BY CHOICE

A Study of Converts to Reform and Conservative Judaism

Brenda Forster, Ph.D.
Department of Sociology
Elmhurst College
Elmhurst, Illinois

and

Joseph Tabachnik, Rabbi Emeritus
West Suburban Temple Har Zion
River Forest, Illinois

Ktav Publishing House, Inc.
Hoboken, New Jersey
1991

Library of Congress Cataloging-in-Publication Data

Forster, Brenda
    Jews by choice : a study of converts to Reform and Conservative
Judaism / Brenda Forster and Joseph Tabachnik.
        p.   cm.
    Includes bibliographical references.
    ISBN 0-88125-383-9
    1. Proselytes and proselyting, Jewish—Case studies.
2. Interfaith marriage—Illinois—Chicago—Case studies.   3. Reform
Judaism—Illinois—Chicago—Case studies.   4. Conservative Judaism-
-Illinois—Chicago—Case studies.   5. Jews—Illinois—Chicago—Case
studies.   I. Tabachnik, Joseph.   II. Title.
BM729.P7F67   1991
296.7'1—dc20   91-14555
                                                                                    CIP

Manufactured in the United States of America

Dedicated to all those who have chosen to join the Jewish people and especially to all those who participated in our study.

—B. Forster

Dedicated in grateful recognition of Judd and Marjorie Weinberg, who helped make possible the publication of this book, and to my *Eshet Hayel*, Miriam, whose constant encouragement brought this volume to fruition.

—J. Tabachnik

TABLE OF CONTENTS

Preface   xi
  Background to the Book   xi
  Reader Focus   xii
  Structure of the Book   xiii
  Terminology   xiv
  Reader Issues   xvii
  Acknowledgments   xviii

**1. Patterns and Issues of U.S. Jewish-Christian
Intermarriage and of Gentile Conversion to Judaism**   1
  Trends in U.S. Jewish Intermarriage   1
  Issues for the Jewish Community about Intermarriage   5
  Trends in U.S. Conversions to Judaism and in
    Intermarriage Identity   8
  Summary of Patterns and Issues   9

**2. Rabbinic Concerns and Rulings about Conversion to
Judaism**   12
  Introduction   12
  Biblical Period   13
    Patriarchal Period   13
    Early Israelite Period   15
    End of the Biblical Period   19
  Talmudic Period   23
  Post-Talmudic Period   31
  Modern Period   36
  Conclusion   51
  Summary of Rabbinic Concerns   52

3. **Summary Findings for Participants in the Chicago Area Introduction to Judaism Course**   54

Introduction   54

History of the Introduction to Judaism Course   54

Study Design   58

Patterns in Convert Backgrounds, Beliefs, and Practices   63

Patterns in Convert Backgrounds   64

Patterns in Convert Background PUSH Factors   65

Patterns in Convert Background PULL Factors   70

Reason for Interest in Conversion of Gentile Partners   74

Patterns in Study Experiences and Conversion Reasons   79

Patterns in Effects of Conversion   80

Patterns in Beliefs of Converts   86

Patterns in Convert Knowledge   88

Major Patterns of Religious Practices   91

Jewish Religious Practices   91

Christian Religious Practices   94

Major Jewish Ethnic Involvements   95

Major Patterns of Child Socialization   98

Summary of Participants' Findings   106

Background Characteristics   106

Convert Adherence to Jewish Beliefs and Practices   106

Jewish Ethnic Beliefs and Involvements   107

Plans for Child Socialization   107

Additional Considerations   107

4. **Convert Comparisons with Partners and Other Born Jews**   109

Patterns in Partner Background Characteristics   109

Parental PUSH Influences   110

Individual PUSH Influences   113

Parental PULL Influences   114

Individual PULL Influences   117

Comparisons Among Groups   120

Background PUSH Variables   121

Background PULL Variables   122

Belief Variables   122

Knowledge Variables   125

Religious Practices   126

Ethnic Involvements 127
Child Socialization Plans 127
Comparison of Our Data with Other Studies 128
Practice Comparisons 128
Ethnic Comparisons 131
Stability of the Couple's Relationship 134
Summary of Comparisons 135

5. Conclusions and Recommendations 138
Conclusions 138
Recommendations 141

Appendix: Supplemental Tables for Chapter 4 155
Table 4.3: Comparisons Among Born Jews', Partners',
and Converts' Background Push Factors 156
Table 4.4: Comparisons Among Born Jews', Partners',
and Converts' Background Pull Factors 158
Table 4.5: Comparisons Among Born Jews', Partners',
and Converts' Belief Patterns 160
Table 4.6: Comparison Among Student Perceptions of
Jewish Beliefs, Students' Own Beliefs, and Actual
Beliefs of Partners and Born Jews 162
Table 4.7: Comparisons Among Born Jews', Partners',
and Converts' Knowledge 164
Table 4.8: Comparisons Among Born Jews', Partners',
and Converts' Patterns of Regular Jewish Religious
Practices 166
Table 4.9: Comparisons Among Born Jews', Partners',
and Converts' Regular Christian Religious Practices 168
Table 4.10: Comparisons Among Born Jews', Partners',
and Converts' Involvements in the Jewish
Community 170
Table 4.11: Comparisons Among Born Jews', Partners',
and Converts' Commitment to Jewish Child-Rearing
Focuses 172

Bibliography 175

Preface

BACKGROUND TO THE BOOK

Only recently has the Jewish community placed the problem of conversion and of converts on its agenda. Converts to Judaism find themselves and their roles in the middle of a serious controversy about dangers to the continued existence of Judaism and of Jews. The debates on various aspects of the issues involving converts are passionate, heated, and complex. On one hand is the possibility of fracturing the religious community's unity over what is labeled the "Who is a Jew?" question. On the other hand is the equally intense debate over how to stop the advance of assimilation as increasing numbers of Jews become secular and then drop from the community that currently comprises only about 2.5 percent of the U.S. population. Added to the concern about dissolution of the community is the fact that even those Jews who are identified with the community seem to evidence a pattern of decline both in religious practice and in Jewish community involvement. Intermarriage between Jew and gentile is used by both optimists and pessimists to argue their view on predicting assimilation. Increasing intermarriage is seen by pessimists as an indication of continuing out-migration of Jews, and by optimists, looking to the increase in gentile conversions, as an indication of a needed infusion into the Jewish community. The issues of intermarriage and of converts are inexorably linked, since the majority of converts (more than 90 percent) are seriously involved with a Jewish partner at the time they seek conversion. As these philosophical and anecdotal debates rage, they are supported by meager statistics. Since only a handful of studies have focused on converts to Judaism, little is known about the actual roles and effects of converts in Judaism.

As a Conservative rabbi who participated in the development of the Introduction to Judaism course for potential converts to Judaism in the Chicago area, Rabbi Tabachnik found himself trying to defend the value of conversion and the positive contribution of converts. His synagogue drew many families with converts into its congregation, and as he saw the converts' growth and positive effects first hand, he became convinced of the need for a well-designed study to provide useful data on converts to the Jewish community. As a sociologist and as a convert to Judaism married to a convert, Dr. Forster had personally experienced some of the difficulties faced by converts and was keenly interested in documenting the experiences of converts. As a member of West Suburban Temple Har Zion, River Forest, Illinois, she had opportunities to interact with Rabbi Tabachnik. When asked, she readily agreed to collaborate with Rabbi Tabachnik on the study leading to this book.

In their joint endeavor, Rabbi Tabachnik made arrangements with the Chicago Association of Reform Rabbis and the Chicago Region of the Rabbinical Assembly, who since 1973 have jointly sponsored the Introduction to Judaism course for potential converts, to permit access to the addresses of past students and to classes enrolling students during 1987 and 1988. He made the resources of West Suburban Temple Har Zion available for mailing the questionnaires and convinced several members to volunteer their services to handle the mailings and to enter questionnaire data for computer analysis. He gained benefactors whose financial contributions supported the mailings and publication costs. He participated in designing the questionnaire and made various other contacts to aid the study's progress. And he took responsibility for researching information on biblical and rabbinical views about conversion. As part of his research, Rabbi Tabachnik gained a unique insight into a sociological principle that over the millennia seems to underlie the rabbis' decisions about the inclusion or exclusion of converts to the community.

Dr. Forster used her research and sociological skills to design the study, questionnaire, and data analysis formats. She drew on her experiences as a convert to develop the practical concerns that guide the approach of this book.

READER FOCUS

Early in the development of the study, we agreed that the book we would publish as one outcome of our study would be written to attract a wide readership, not just researchers or religious studies experts. Our concern was to provide a book that would not only present the specific findings of our study of current and former participants in the Introduction to Judaism course but also provide both sociological and religious contexts for the issues being debated. It is our hope that this book will interest born Jews, Jews by choice, intermarrieds, and prospective converts. As we previously indicated, the Jewish community is engaged in a debate about assimilation, intermarriage, and conversion. We hope this book will provide needed clarity to the facts and issues for born Jews who are directly involved as intermarrieds or as relatives of intermarrieds and for born Jews who are more indirectly involved as parties in the debate over the direction and form the community will take in the years to come. We also hope the book will aid those who have joined the Jewish community as intermarrieds, as converts, or as potential members. We perceive a need for non-Jews who attach themselves to the Jewish fold to understand the social and religious context in which their role is enacted. Understanding the Jewish community's concerns about the role of gentiles by birth should help highlight the issues converts and mixed-marrieds need to address if they desire a positive, committed, and useful attachment. Both groups, we hope, will find the data we provide interesting and beneficial.

Because we wish our material to be accessible to this wider audience of born Jews and of joiners, we have developed our presentation using easily understandable terminology and data formats. We do provide the reader with major references to aid further reading, but we have chosen to present ideas and themes rather than an extensive review of previous writings and research on our topics. We also provide chapter overviews and summaries so the reader will not lose track of the major concerns we will be addressing in our analysis.

STRUCTURE OF THE BOOK

The five chapters in this book are intended to lead the reader through the issues, to the data, and on to some practicalities that flow from this discussion. Chapter 1 introduces the U.S. Jewish community intermarriage situation and gives information on the patterns and controversies surrounding Jewish-gentile intermarriage and gentile conversion. This will provide a context for the reader to understand our data. Chapter 2 provides a synopsis of the four-thousand-year period (biblical and rabbinical) in which Jews have struggled with the role of outsiders who seek to join the Jewish family. We feel this information is needed both to provide a summary of rabbinical concerns and procedures that is not available elsewhere and to form the framework for analyzing and interpreting our data. Chapter 3 describes the study design and findings on the experiences of enrolled and former participants in the Introduction to Judaism course in Chicago, with an emphasis on actual converts to Judaism. Chapter 4 presents a comparison of main beliefs and practices of a sample of Reform and Conservative born Jews, the Jewish partners of the gentiles by birth, and the Introduction to Judaism participants. Chapter 5 gives a summary of the concerns raised throughout the book and offers our conclusions and recommendations. Tables to provide quick summaries of major points and of the data appear as needed throughout the book. It is our hope that the tables will be readable, interesting, and useful in their own right.

TERMINOLOGY

Before we proceed with our discussion, we need to explain something about the terminology we will be using throughout the book.

The words conversion and convert are actually gentile terms referring to a change in religious belief, identification, and practice. Particularly in Chapter 2, we will use various Hebrew terms that convey more the sense of identification with a people than with a religious system. The biblical term *ger* is the earliest designation of an outsider as "a stranger who resided in the midst of Jews;" later the term *ger zedek* (righteous alien-stranger) was applied to gentiles who identified with Judaism. The terms *proselyte* and *proselytism* are the concepts used officially in Jewish sources such as the *Encyclopedia Judaica*. The word *proselyte* comes from a Greek word meaning "to approach or to come to." And the terms conversion, proselytism, and missionizing primarily refer to the process of a religious community seeking to make members of outsiders. The latter two terms convey an active outreach by the community to "entice" outsiders to join. Added to these various terms used to describe the person and the process of gaining group membership is the recently coined term *Jew by choice*, which some prefer to the term convert.

Another set of terms referring to marriage between Jews and gentiles causes problems in understanding for outsiders. The terms reflect the ambivalent attitude toward themselves that converts encounter in the Jewish community. In Christian circles, a person from outside the faith or denomination who converts is considered a full member, loses all former identifications, and when counted is considered a Catholic, or Baptist, or Lutheran, or whatever. And when that person marries an insider, the marriage is considered of one faith, not as an interfaith marriage. Not so in Judaism, as we will discuss in more detail in Chapter 1. Marriages between a convert to Judaism and a Jew are still considered intermarriages by Jews. Only occasionally and in technical discussions is a distinction recognized between mixed intermarriages in which the gentile spouse does not convert and conversionary intermarriages in which the gentile spouse converts to Judaism.

We have elected to use the term *gentile* in our discussion as the category for all those not born Jews, though occasionally we use the term non-Jew. We are aware that they are generalization terms that mask many potentially important distinctions among out-group members; that is, some gentiles may be more acceptable to Jews than others, some more attracted to Judaism than others. But such distinctions are not our concern here. We felt that the term *gentile* was less judgmental and more universally used than the term *non-Jew*. We also focus our discussion on Jewish-Christian (mainline Protestant and Catholic) relationships because the majority of U.S. intermarriages with Jews are with spouses from Christian backgrounds. There are Jewish-Moslem, Jewish-Hindu, Jewish-Buddhist, and other such unions, but they are scarce, and little is known of them. Generally speaking, Jewish-gentile intermarriages are racially homogenous—white. (In the United States, Semites of northern European extraction are considered white.) An estimated 6 percent of Jewish-Gentile conversionary unions are racially mixed (black, oriental, Asian, Indian, Hispanic, and so on); two-thirds of these partners convert to Reform Judaism because of its outreach efforts (Gallob, 1990). Again, little is known of these special situations. Therefore, our discussion addresses the majority intermarried situation of born Jew with a white, Christian, gentile spouse who may be a convert to Judaism.

In speaking of gentiles who seek attachment to a born Jew and/or Judaism, we will use several terms including *non-Jewish partner, gentile spouse, potential convert,* and *student.* We also use the terms *out-marriage, mixed marriage,* and *intermarriage* basically interchangeably to refer to Jewish-gentile marriages, since all these terms are used in the literature. *Out-marriage* is more commonly used by sociologists along with the term *exogamous; intermarriage* is the more generally used term.

Another point to which the reader should be alerted and that we discuss in our subsequent chapters is the need to address both a religious and an ethnic dimension in the relationship of the gentile within the Jewish community. To a Christian, the focus of conversion is a religious one. Religious conversion in a marriage context is an accepted model among religious Christians. Only in vague notions of close family bonds and Jewish cohesiveness with perhaps a bit of awareness of Jewish humor does a modern U.S. gentile generally apprehend the ethnic domain that is as important to Jewish identity and definition as religious practice, perhaps more so. It is relatively easier for a sincere gentile to practice Judaism than it is to be a recognized and respected member of the Jewish community. It is difficult for a gentile to absorb ethnic empathy, commitment, and self-identification, to speak of we, us, and our when speaking of Jews. We trace the long-term Jewish concern with both dimensions in the discussion that follows. In order to make clearer what we will call the ethnic, cultural, or peoplehood domain, Figure 2.1, pages 49–50, provides a brief summary of major differences between U.S. Jews and the Christian gentile majority. Most of the differences are ethnic (sociocultural) in nature.

Generally for simplicity we will use the term *Jews* and *Jewish community* in our discussions. However, historically the ancestors of the people now called Jews have been variously called by themselves and by others—for example, Israelites, Hebrews, tribes, and sons of the Patriarchs. Modern Jewish issues are rooted in the experiences of these ancestors, and in Chapter 2 we discuss historical differences and changes for each of the major periods as the Jewish people evolved. We also speak of Judaism, which is a religious identification fostered by the rabbis in diaspora (the exiled or by-choice life of Jews outside the land of Israel). The modern religion of Judaism contains only prayers as correlates of the earlier sacrificial religion. Other religious identifications usually applied by outsiders have focused on the people as worshipers of the One God, as People of the Covenant, as Chosen People (chosen by God for his personal Revelation), and as People of the Book. When we speak of religious leaders and experts, we acknowledge the fact that the rabbis have built their rulings on the traditions of the prophets before them, who built on the work of the priests, and judges, who gained inheritance from Moses and the Patriarchs. In identifying the various time periods involved in the development of the Jewish people and Judaism, we will use the abbreviations BCE (Before the Common Era) and CE (Common Era) rather than the Christian-oriented BC (Before Christ) and AD (Year of the Lord).

Another consideration for the reader and for converts especially is the difference between Christians and Jews in emphasis on beliefs and behavior. Christians stress issues of belief as central to their relationship to God while Jews stress actions as a member of a covenantal community. Religiously oriented Christians who seek to learn about Judaism whether in the writings of Jews or through courses such as Introduction to Judaism find discussions on the proper rituals for observing the holidays but precious little about Jewish tenets. Jews do have beliefs that can be characterized as theological, but traditionally these beliefs are implicit in action-oriented considerations. In introducing new members to the faith community, Jews begin with the history (experiences and practices) of Jews from Abraham to the present while Christians begin with faith (belief) propositions based on the death and resurrection of the person they call Christ. We will discuss the relevance of the practice versus belief emphasis further in Chapters 3 and 4.

The reader may also notice that our spelling of Hebrew terms is different from spellings used elsewhere. Transliteration (representation of Hebrew letters and pronunciations in English) is not standardized. For example, the world *Hanukah* is also spelled *Hanukkah, Chanukah,* and *Chanukkah* depending on the source. We have tried to use the simplest and most common form and then stick to it for consistency. We also italicize all but the most commonly known Hebrew terms.

Finally, we will use the term *assimilation* to refer to the adherence of born Jews to the larger gentile culture, which in the extreme means that either they or their children lose their identities as Jews. We will use the term *absorption* to refer to the integration of gentiles into the Jewish community in such a way that either they or their children become fully recognized and participate as Jews.

With these complexities in mind, we proceed with our discussion.

READER ISSUES

In reading the pages that follow, the reader may wish to ponder the following questions:

- In what context have issues of assimilation into the gentile community versus absorption of gentiles into the Jewish community arisen over the years?
- What is similar and what is different about the modern U.S. context of concerns about intermarriages and conversion and other periods?
- What procedures for admission of gentiles to Judaism have been established over the millennia?
- What behaviors are expected of converts in the religious domain and in the ethnic (sociocultural) domain?
- What are the religious and ethnic beliefs and behaviors evidenced by converts to Judaism?
- How do the beliefs and practices of converts to Judaism compare with born Jews, with their Jewish spouses, and with gentiles who intermarry without conversion to Judaism?
- What concerns should the current U.S. Jewish community address if it wishes to aid the absorption of converts, including their Jewish identification and participation?
- What issues need to be addressed if the children of Jewish-gentile intermarriages are to identify and involve themselves as Jews and to pass that participation on to their children?

ACKNOWLEDGEMENTS

A project of this size requires the support of many people, not just the authors. The Chicago Association of Reform Judaism and the Chicago Region of the Rabbinical Assembly, who jointly sponsor the Introduction to Judaism course, provided us access to both former and current students. We had the help of pretesters, born Jews, Jewish partners, and current and former students in the Introduction to Judaism course who were gracious enough to take the time needed to answer our lengthy questionnaire. We had office help from the staff of West Suburban Temple Har Zion, River Forest, Illinois, to organize and conduct our mailing. Both Doris Levin and Lucy Matz became involved as staff members. We were blessed with the volunteer help of several members of West Suburban Temple Har Zion to complete our mailing operation. Bernice Sheft spent hours and hours as the manager of the mailing operation. With the help of various women in the temple, Bernice completed the exacting task of tracking down current names and addresses of former students; folding, stuffing, and labeling the questionnaire mailings;

keeping records on returns; and doing follow-up mailings. Barry Weiss used his computer services to prepare our mailing labels. Maxine Horwich spent months entering the questionnaire data onto computer disks for entry to our computer. Russel Forster, Brenda's son, acted as research assistant and data processor. His knowledge and skill at running the SPSSX package on the Harris 800 system at Elmhurst College got the massive amount of data we obtained into shape. Kari Busch aided the work in transcribing the data from printouts to summary sheets. Rita Kuta, Brenda's sister, provided the needed word processing expertise to prepare the various questionnaries and manuscripts. We are also indebted to David Stadt and to Miriam Tabachnik for their support.

The librarians at Spertus College of Judaica, Chicago, particularly Dan Sharon and Yehoshua Ben Avraham, aided us in finding the necessary sources for our discussions in Chapter 1 and Chapter 2. Dr. Monford Harris and Dr. Byron Sherwin, also of Spertus College, read early drafts of portions of this book and gave invaluable suggestions.

A special recognition goes to Rabbi William Frankel of Northfield, Illinois, whose knowledge of rabbinics and keen perception of American Jewish life influenced our thinking.

Finally, without the generous financial contributions of Judd and Marjorie Weinberg and Alvin Gottlieb this project would not have gotten off the ground. We acknowledge with gratitude that their generosity supported the questionnaire, data analysis, manuscript preparation, and publication phases for this book. We are indeed fortunate that they believed in the importance of this endeavor and were willing to underwrite much of this project.

To all who aided us, we extend our appreciation.

1

Patterns and Issues of U.S. Jewish-Christian Intermarriage and of Gentile Conversion to Judaism

FROM THE POINT of view of the Jewish community, intermarriage of Jews with gentiles is the main concern and not conversion. As we indicated in the Preface, even where there is conversion of the gentile partner to Judaism, Jews still consider the marriage an intermarriage. Therefore, while our book is about converts, we have to begin with a discussion of Jewish concerns about intermarriage in order to understand their reaction to conversion and to converts.

In this chapter we will examine trends of intermarriage in the United States. Then we will turn our attention to current U.S. trends in conversion to Judaism. This discussion will provide the context for the concerns to which our study responds.

TRENDS IN U.S. JEWISH INTERMARRIAGE

To get some idea of the importance of and effect of Jewish intermarriage in the United States, one must look at the historical patterns and trends. The data presented here are drawn from a mixed bag of sources—government statistics, local Jewish community studies, and a few national studies. Since the data are spotty and often not easily comparable, one must use great caution not to take the numbers as absolute. At the same time, the data suggest patterns and trends and are all that is available. Eleven major Jewish community studies tend to be cited in the literature: Los Angeles 1986, Denver 1981, American Jewish Committee (Egon Mayer)

1

1976, National Jewish Population Study 1971, Boston 1965, Providence 1963, NORC 1961, Indiana 1959, San Francisco 1958, Washington 1956, and Iowa 1953. Only three of these studies used a national sample, and the Indiana and Iowa data are from government data on rather small, atypical Jewish populations. In the discussion that follows, we will give the data source only when it is particularly relevant. Most of the published reports on the Jewish community and on intermarriage provide pattern information and estimates of trends without giving the data source. In addition, estimates from different studies vary somewhat in their projection of patterns.

The first U.S. Jewish intermarriage was recorded in 1660, only six years after Jews first came to New Amsterdam (Mayer, 1985, p. 78). Because of an unbalanced sex ratio in the colonial period, it is estimated that from 1776 to 1840 the intermarriage rate was 28.7 percent (Stern, 1967, pp. 142–143). However, once there was an influx of Jewish immigrants in the early 1900s, the rate dropped to 1.2 percent. From 1900 to 1940, the intermarriage rate was 2 percent to 4 percent, and from 1940 to 1950 it was 5 percent to 6 percent (Silberman, 1985, p. 287). Until the 1960s, the intermarriage rate for Jews was below 10 percent. A study by Rosenthal (1963) of Iowa data indicated that Jews in small Jewish communities had a considerably higher rate of intermarriage than those in concentrated communities (36.3 percent in 1953 and 53.6 percent in 1959).

By the late 1950s, while Jewish centers had lower intermarriage rates than small communities, their rates were also increasing. The Washington study in 1956 showed a 13.1 percent intermarriage rate of which 9.4 percent were Jewish males out-marrying and 4.5 percent were Jewish females (Rosenthal, 1963, p. 16). By 1965 in Boston the rate had risen to 20 percent (Schwartz, 1970, p. 110), and by the early 1970s the estimates were of a 32 percent rate (Mayer and Sheingold, 1979, p. 2). Interestingly, the 1986 Los Angeles study showed a 20.2 percent rate (17 percent to a Christian partner, 3.2 percent to partners of other backgrounds) (Sandberg, 1986, p. 53). It appears that while the intermarriage rate has been increasing overall, currently it is about one-fifth (20 percent) rather than the commonly accepted one-third (33 percent).

A qualification to this lower figure must be made, however. The 20 percent rate represents an average of all generations. Some research indicates that the rate varies by generation. Sandberg found in the Los Angeles study that the first generation (foreign-born) intermarriage rate was 11.6 percent, the children of immigrants had a 12.7 percent rate, the third generation rate was 28.8 percent, and the fourth generation rate was 43.5 percent (1986, p. 140). Since Los Angeles has a large Jewish community, the finding of an almost 50 percent intermarriage rate for great-grandchildren of immigrants is unsettling, since that generation is both large and influential in determining the future for the Jewish community. Even more alarming, a 1988 study by social scientists at Brandeis University found an out-marriage rate of 72 percent for current eighteen- to twenty-nine-year-old Jews (Gallob, 1988, p. 27).

As a comparison, the rate of Jewish intermarriage, while of great concern to the Jewish community, has remained well below the intermarriage rates for other religious and ethnic groups. In 1957, a voluntary population survey conducted by the U.S. government showed 7.2 percent of existing marriages in which one marital partner was Jewish and the other gentile, whereas 21.5 percent of those involving Catholics were interdenominational intermarriages. The rate for Protestant interdenominational marriages was 8.6 percent in the 1930s (Baron, 1952) but was 30 percent to 40 percent by the 1950s. Today out-marriage rates for Christians (marrying across denominations) is greater than 50 percent. The comparatively lower rate for Jews, which was maintained for a longer period than for other religious groups (20 percent to 30 percent for Christian groups by the 1950s but not until the 1980s for Jews), reflects stronger ethnic-family-peoplehood ties present in the Jewish community than in the Christian community. However, because of their significantly smaller size, losses of members are a more serious threat to the continued survival of a Jewish community in the United States and worldwide. Therefore, Jews show greater concern than do Christian groups about the effect of loss of members. Christian denominations also have the advantage that out-marriage of their members is to other Christian denominations. So, for example, loss of a Catholic in marriage to a Lutheran is still not a loss for Christendom, whereas marriage of a Jew to a Christian is more likely to lead to a permanent loss for the Jewish community. We will return to this issue in the next section.

Consequently, a 7.2 percent loss rate in the late 1950s, though low by today's standards, began to agitate some in the Jewish community. The figure had doubled since the immigrant generation. In December 1964, the Commission on Synagogue Relations and the Federation of Jewish Philanthropies in New York sponsored a conference on "Intermarriage and the Future of the American Jew." Significantly, only some of the participants mentioned the possibility of initiating programs so gentile partners could convert; the others outlined programs on prevention. In a summary of the proceedings, Graenum Berger spoke about "arresting" and "preventing" intermarriage (1964, p. 159).

As the rate of intermarriage increased significantly in the 1960s, data from the "National Jewish Population Study," conducted by the Council of Jewish Federation and Welfare, were released in 1971. The findings stunned the Jewish community. From 1961 to 1965, the rate of intermarriage had risen to 17.4 percent, and, from 1966 to 1971, by some widely accepted estimates the rate had climbed to 31.7 percent. (Though, as we previously stated, some experts believe a 20 percent rate to be a more accurate estimate.)

The steep increase was due to many factors. It seems that Jews had completed the naturalization process begun by the immigrant generation and, therefore, had shed their immigrant ties. The sharp increase in intermarriage was also the result of other factors in the American environment. The civil rights struggle and subsequent legislation enacted by Congress in 1964 forbade discrimination in employment, and the quota systems in universities that discriminated against Jews were abolished, while corporations opened their doors to minority groups including Jews. Jews left their parental homes and began to enroll in universities that had been closed to them previously; many joined corporate life, which entailed mobility. The feminist revolution opened careers for women that made it possible for them to lead a less sheltered existence that, in turn, led to broader socialization with people of the opposite sex.

The memories of Christian persecution, so traumatic to the older generation, were no longer relevant to many young people. Jews acquired gentile friends and began to experience an openness in American life. The church likewise began to encourage an openness to other faiths. Pope John XXIII, after Vatican II, which, according to him, "opened a window to the world," urged the church to increase interdenominational contacts that included Jews and to broaden social contacts.

In view of these pressures toward greater intermarriage, the Jewish community could no longer ignore the possibility of attrition due to intermarriage. What to do about it become an item of priority of the Jewish agenda.

In 1973, Rabbi Schindler, the president of the Union of American Hebrew Congregations, the lay body of the Reform movement, called for "a positive effort to come to grips with the problem of intermarriage, to contain the loss of our numerical strength which it threatens, and, if at all possible, to convert the loss into a gain." With concern for the next generation of Jews, Schindler called for attempts to ensure "that the majority of the children issuing from such marriages, will in fact be reared as Jews. . . . We need to stop bemoaning our fate, to shake off once and for all the defensive stand, born out of a ghetto mentality, and to make Judaism a proud and assertive faith."

Intermarriage does not occur without prior dating contact, since in the United States people use dating as the mechanism for mate selection. Sandberg found differences in teen out-dating depending on Jewish religious affiliation as follows: Orthodox 39 percent, Conservative 62 percent, and Reform 67 percent. These rates increase somewhat to 51 percent, 74 percent, and 85 percent for Jewish individuals no longer living with their parents. Los Angeles Jews showed little resistance in their stated reactions should their own child intermarry. Intermarriage for their own child was opposed by only 38 percent of the Orthodox, 16 percent of Conservatives, and 12 percent of the Reform congregants (Sandberg, 1986, p. 54). As our later discussion will show, this acceptance of intermarriage is a rather new phenomenon and certainly gives doomsayers a basis for their prophecies.

Having looked at the patterns in intermarriage, we briefly turn our attention to a further specification of the vital issues intermarriage raises for the Jewish community.

ISSUES FOR THE JEWISH COMMUNITY ABOUT INTERMARRIAGE

Intermarriage has been viewed as a perennial danger to Jewish validity and continuity (Rosenman cited by Silberman, 1985, p. 286).

Intermarriage is a holocaust of our own making (Rabbi Sol Roth cited by Silberman, 1985, p. 286).

The hydra-headed monster of assimilation takes on many forms, the most menacing of which is intermarriage (Robert Gordis cited by Silberman, 1985, p. 285).

The topic of Jewish intermarriage (especially of Jewish-Christian intermarriage, the most frequent kind) and the related subtopic of conversion and of converts to Judaism touches a root nerve in the Jewish psyche. Intermarriage is invariably tied to intense fears of the demise of the Jewish community through assimilation into the dominant culture. Intermarriage, according to the worst scenario, is the next to last step for Jews moving out of the Jewish community.

Recent discussions reflecting on the survival chances of the Jewish community seem to fall into one of two camps—assimilationists/pessimists or transformationists/optimists (Glazer, 1987, p. 14). The pessimists claim that trends associated with modernism, secularization, and assimilation will cause the demise of the Jewish community in the United States over the next several decades. They point to several demographic indicators. The percentage of Jews in the U.S. population is falling. In 1880, Jews were 0.5 percent of the U.S. population, in 1930 3.7 percent, but in 1984 2.5 percent (approximately 5.5 million). This now falling percentage is affected by a decrease in Jewish immigration to the U.S. (even Russian immigration is now redirected to Israel), a falling Jewish birth rate (1.5 in 1965 and 0.7 in 1975) that is well below even replacement level, and a rising intermarriage rate (7 percent in the 1940s, 17 percent in the 1960s, and an estimated 20 percent to 32 percent in the 1980s) (Goldstein, 1987, p. 131). Add to these decreases the rising mortality rate of an aging Jewish population and the "passing" of an unknown number of born Jews to whom identify as a Jew is meaningless at best and a detriment at worst. (Orthodox commentators would include the "falling away" from *halachic* Judaism of Conservative, Reform, and Reconstructionist Jews as also indicting steps toward the demise of the Jewish community.) Most pessimists also include the lack of intensive Jewish education for the majority of Jewish children and delay of marriage in twenty-five to thirty-four-year-olds (98 percent married in the 1960s, 74 percent in the 1970s) (Goldstein, 1987, p. 137). (A delay in marriage is also associated with lower birth rates.) In the 1960s Sklare was one of the first to sound the alarm about the decreasing U.S. Jewish population. He particularly pointed to intermarriage as the main problem, because,

> in its collective aspects intermarriage menaces the continuity of the group. In its individual aspects, it menaces the continuity of generations within the family, the ability of family members

to identify with one another, and the satisfaction of such members with their family roles (Sklare, 1971, p. 182).

The optimists, on the other hand, while viewing similar data, come to different conclusions about the future for the Jewish community and about the meaning and effect of intermarriage. For the optimists, while the Jewish population is proportionally decreasing, 5.5 million is still a large community. They point to recent evidence that fourth-generation Jews desire larger families than their parents and to the fact that a high education and occupational status no longer means a decrease in family size. (Unlike their gentile counterparts, upper status Jewish females have larger than replacement-size families.) While optimists agree that intermarriage is a factor to be considered, they believe the actual rates to be about 24 percent (Silberman, 1985, p. 293), and they point out that some 20 percent to 50 percent of gentile spouses eventually convert to Judaism (one-third is the usually accepted estimate). According to Mayer, the major researcher on intermarriage, the rate of conversion to Judaism went up 300 percent during the last twenty years but may now be falling (1983, p. 58). During the 1970s, some 7,000 to 8,000 people per year converted to Judaism, with Jews by choice comprising an estimated 2 percent to 4 percent (about 100,000) of all Jews. Optimists believe these "imports" counterbalance losses to the community. The optimists argue that while there has been a decrease in traditional Jewish practices by most Jews, there is near universal observance of Passover and Hanukah, a very high participation in Rosh Hashanah and Yom Kippur, and a strong commitment to Israel (Glazer, 1987, p. 14). Three-fourths of Jews still identify with a "denomination" (Goldscheider, 1987, p. 278), and most Jews indicate that the majority of their friends are Jews. According to one optimist:

The Jewish community in America has changed, indeed has been transformed [by modernization]. But, in that process, it has survived as a dynamic source of networks and resources binding together family, friends, and neighbors, ethnically and religiously—in every way the American Jewish community represents for Jews and other ethnic minorities a paragon of continuity and change in modern pluralistic society (Goldscheider, 1987, p. 280).

In sum, the controversy over intermarriage then represents the core concern of the Jewish community, which lost one-third of its members recently in the Holocaust. Is intermarriage the final step before assimilation? Do conversionary intermarrieds contribute to the strengthening or to the dissolution of the practice of Judaism and of Jewish identity? What about the offspring of intermarrieds—are they lost to the Jewish community? We hope our study will shed some light on these questions.

Having looked at the patterns of Jewish intermarriage and having considered the issues those patterns raise, we turn our attention to the specific concern of this book—conversion to Judaism. What do we know about the patterns in conversion to Judaism?

TRENDS IN U.S. CONVERSIONS TO JUDAISM AND IN INTERMARRIAGE IDENTITY

As debates and concerns about Jewish intermarriage have arisen, another change has complicated the Jewish-gentile intermarriage picture—conversion to Judaism by the gentile (usually Christian) partner. Although the first conversion in the United States took place in 1763 in Philadelphia (Mayer, 1985, p. 90), before the 1960s conversion to Judaism by the gentile partner was exceedingly rare. By the 1980s, Mayer and others estimate that about one-third of the gentile spouses are converting to Judaism, while another 20 percent, although they do not convert, still identify themselves as Jewish (1987, p. 90). Ten percent of the Jewish spouses convert to their gentile partner's religion, and 17 percent reject all religious identity (Mayer, 1987, p. 214). While this latter 27 percent are lost to the Jewish community, the remaining three-quarters of intermarrieds retain ties and identification with Judaism and the Jewish community.

The 1961 NORC study calculated an intermarriage loss rate according to the partner's religious identity. It was found that in Protestant-Jewish marriages, 66 percent of the Jewish male partners and 58 percent of the Jewish female partners retained their identity, producing a loss rate of 20 percent; Catholic-Jewish intermarriages produced retention rates of 62 percent and 53 percent, respectively, or a Jewish loss rate of 26 percent. In intermarriages where both partners disavow a religious identification, 38 percent of the Jewish males and 50 percent of the Jewish females retain an ethnic Jewish identity with a loss rate of 47 percent. Overall, 55 percent of Jews intermarrying retain their Jewish identification (Schwartz, 1970, p. 112). It is the larger group of Jewish-identified conversionary couples that we will focus on in our subsequent discussion.

According to Mayer, for the one-third of gentile partners who convert to Judaism, 15 percent convert before meeting their partner, 40 percent convert before marriage, 23 percent convert before the birth of the first child, and 22 percent convert at other times (1985, p. 235). Mayer also indicates that partners of a Catholic background are least likely to convert, then those with no religious identity, then those from a Protestant faith, and most likely to convert are liberal Protestants whose own parents were part of an intermarriage (1985, p. 230). Ninety percent of converts to Judaism are females (Mayer as quoted by Gallob, 1985, p. 20). As we shall see in Chapter 3, our data show similar patterns.

In an attempt to distinguish the various combinations of inter-marrieds, the terms *mixed* and *conversionary* or *mitzvah* marriages are used. As we previously stated, it should be noted here that other religious groups do not consider couples as intermarried when the nonmember converts. The Jewish community, however, is uncomfortable about converts, not accepting them as "real" Jews and expressing concern as to how much they will "water down" Jewish practices and/or import Christian or other observances into the marriage. Consequently, the term *intermarried* is used for all couples where one partner was not born Jewish. Mayer proposed four categories of intermarrieds: (1) Assimilationists (10 percent), where the born Jew converts to the partner's religion; (2) Rejectionists (17 percent), where the partners reject any religious identity; (3) Conversionist (33 percent), where the gentile converts to Judaism; and (4) Integrationist (40 percent), where neither partner converts, but they try to blend observances from both backgrounds (1985, p. 282). The chart in Figure 1.1 graphically presents these various combinations of intermarriage.

SUMMARY OF PATTERNS AND ISSUES

To summarize, the data indicate that the general Jewish intermarriage rate has increased since 1960 from less than 10 percent to about 20 percent (some say 32 percent). The rates are higher for native-born generations, with the fourth generation showing almost a 50 percent rate. In the past, it was primarily Jewish males who

FIGURE 1.1
VARIATIONS IN FORMS OF JEWISH INTERMARRIAGE

Intermarriage Type	Mixed				Conversionary	
Religious Identity	Jew by birth-Gentile No Religious Identity	Christian-Jew Separate Identifications*	Christian-Jew Identifying with Jews	Christian-Jew Convert to Christian**	Jew-Christian Convert to Judaism with Christian Leanings	Jew-Christian Convert to Judaism Fully Jewish-Oriented
Mayer Percentage	17%	20%	20%	10%	33%	
Mayer Term	Rejectionist	Integrationist		Assimilationist	Conversionist	

* We use Christian here for convenience since the majority of intermarriages are Jew-Christian. The categories apply to other religious identifications such as Buddhist-Jew and so on.

** This category is not usually studied since the Jewish community does not consider an out-convert part of the group.

out-married, but currently the ratio of Jewish males to Jewish females out-marrying is nearly equal. Interdating is a growing practice even among Orthodox Jews. Younger Jews of all branches show little rejection of intermarriage for their own children. These patterns suggest serious problems afoot for maintaining the U.S. Jewish community at its current number of 5.5 million.

A possible countering factor is the fact that about one-third of the gentile spouses eventually convert, another 20 percent consider themselves Jews without formal conversion but by commitment, and another quarter seek to maintain some kind of Jewish identity and practice along with the gentile spouse's religion. Only about 20 percent of intermarrieds completely reject Judaism and a Jewish identity. Most converts are females from a liberal Protestant background converting to Reform Judaism.

The various combinations of intermarried identifications are, for simplicity, usually discussed as either mixed or conversionary, which we will do also.

We have shown the matter of Jewish intermarriage to be related to key identity and survival issues for the entire Jewish community. As the rate of out-marriage has continued to increase, Jewish response generally has moved from total rejection, to grudging acceptance, to resignation, and to growth in attempts to react in a positive manner as gentile spouses began to seek conversion in greater numbers.

Before we continue analyzing the issues about the role of converts using our study data, we will turn our attention to rabbinic concerns and policies for conversion over the centuries. Since converts today gain legitimate Jewish identification only through a religious conversion handled by a rabbi, it is imperative that we understand this religious context. It is the rabbis who debate and decide the criteria for admission. To their point of view we now turn our attention.

2

Rabbinic Concerns and Rulings about Conversion to Judaism

INTRODUCTION

We will let the words of the biblical convert Ruth—"Your people shall be my people"—provide the question for our discussion: For Jews, how does "your people become my people?" We begin our investigation of the meaning and process of conversion to Judaism with an examination of the concerns and the procedures established by the rabbis and their precursors. We will be examining a four-thousand-year span in which outsiders became one with the Jewish people.[1]

The discussion of conversion occurs in several major sources—the biblical text itself, various segments of the Talmud, codes, responsa, philosophical literature, and most recently in various rabbinic writings. These various sources will serve as guidelines to our understanding of the problems associated with accepting converts to Judaism. A catalog of the various writings actually leads to what appears to be contradictory decisions—some in favor, some opposed to accepting converts. However, the prevailing notion in our culture today is that Judaism throughout history discouraged proselytism and conversion, a view colored by the influence of the last two thousand years, which have tended to make conversion a difficult process, as we shall see. Since other writers have sought to gather comprehensive information about rulings concerning conversion to Judaism, it is our intention to provide only a summary overview. Two important works on the topic are *Jewish Proselytism in the*

---

1. For simplification we will talk about conversion to Judaism even when we are incorporating the earlier situations of joining the tribes, the Hebrews, and the Israelites.

First Five Centuries of the Common Era (Braude, 1940) and *Proselytism in the Talmudic Period* (Bamberger, 1939).

As we began to research for this book we agreed that we needed a framework in order to make sense of the various authoritative opinions and to aid our data analysis as well. As we looked at the rabbinic sources, we began to see a common, transcending theme. Whether the procedures for joining the Jewish people (including intermarrying) were severe or lenient seemed consistently related to concerns (or lack of them) about the community's ability to absorb outsiders into the group. To make it clear, our conclusion is as follows:

In times when intermarriage tended to lead to the assimilation of Jewish partners into the gentile world, such marriages were strongly discouraged, and the requirements for conversion became demanding.

In times when conditions tended to ensure that the gentile partner would be absorbed by the Jewish community, requirements for conversion were lenient or absent.

Given this rather sociological view of the issue of conversion, our following account and analysis will address three primary concerns for each of the major periods—biblical, talmudic, posttalmudic, and modern. The three issues are: (1) What is the sociohistoric context of the Jewish community, particularly as it relates to the concern about absorption/assimilation? (2) What specific concerns about absorption/assimilation are illustrated? and (3) What are the policies and procedures regulating joining the Jewish people (as best we can determine from the extant records)?

BIBLICAL PERIOD

Patriarchal Period

We begin our discussion with the biblical period, which itself spans approximately 1,500 years. The issue of who absorbs/assimilates whom is evident in the earliest biblical records dealing with marriages in the patriarchal period. The patriarchs and matriarchs were deeply involved with their children's marriage choices. Living in the land of Canaan, they feared that their children would intermarry with the Canaanites and that such marriages would spell the spiritual demise of the nascent Hebrew faith. The Canaanites, being more numerous, would easily assimilate the patriarchal family through such marriages. Thus, Abraham, the first Jew, instructs his servant Eliezer, "You will not take a wife for my son from the daughters of the Canaanites among whom I live, but you will go to the land of my birth and to my own kinfolk and get a wife for my son Isaac" (Genesis 24:3–4). Abraham preferred that his son's wife come from a distant land so that there would be a lesser likelihood of his son's being assimilated by his wife's kindred. The wife's family, removed from their daughter, would not be able to exert a religious influence on the newlyweds, which would be the case if the wife came from one of the neighboring tribes. Had Abraham been mainly concerned that Isaac marry only within his own family, the following dialogue between Abraham and his servant Eliezer would not have been necessary. Eliezer says to Abraham, "What if the woman does not want to come with me to this land, must I take your son back to the land from which you came?" Abraham replies, "On no account should you take my son back there" (Genesis 24:5–6). The issue is not only whom Isaac was going to marry but also where and under what influence he would live. What Abraham feared most was the removal of his son to a distant land where he would come under the influence of a different faith. A wife of Isaac coming from an idolatrous background must not reside near her family who would encourage the idolatry.

Similarly the patriarch Isaac blessed Jacob and charged him, "You shall not marry one of the Canaanite women. Arise, go to Paddan-aram to the house of Bethuel your mother's father, and there choose a wife for yourself from among the daughters of Laban your mother's brother" (Genesis 28:1–2). Jacob marries Rachael and Leah and, despite his fear of his brother Esau, he sees the need to return home, for otherwise his family would be assimilated by Rachael's and Leah's relatives.

The concern in the patriarchal period was understandable. Monotheism was a new religious concept, and there was a justifiable fear that the new faith would be strangled in its infancy by the prevailing idolatrous neighboring civilization. Although Abraham's kin residing in Mesopotamia were also idolators, as we learn from the narrative of Rachael stealing her father's idols (Genesis 31:8–35), nevertheless, since these wives would be taken from their parental environment, they would be distanced from the influence of their family and their native faith. When Esau, the other son of Isaac, marries a nearby Hittite woman not from the family we are told, "and they [the Hittite women] were a source of bitterness to Isaac and Rebecca" (Genesis 26:35). The implied rule for the survival of monotheism in the patriarchal period was to fend off the neighboring culture by keeping children and spouses close to home and above all to avoid marriages with the offspring of nearby tribes.

The patriarchal period can be summed up in the words spoken by Abraham in describing his status: "I am a resident alien among you . . ." (Genesis 23:4). The patriarchs lived among idolators and in order to transmit their new faith to future generations, they set boundaries particularly in marriages between themselves and others lest their children would be assimilated by their neighbors. At this point of development, religious and ethnic (peoplehood, cultural) aspects were congruous, and marriage was the procedure by which one "entered the family" and thereby the religion.

Early Israelite Period

The patriarchal concern was carried over into the premonarchal period when the Israelite tribes reached the promised land after the Exodus from Egypt. The biblical books of Joshua and Judges record constant battles with the neighboring tribes in the land of Canaan, and deep concern about intermarriage was evident. The Bible establishes an outright prohibition of intermarriage with the Canaanites in the early Israelite period: "You must not marry them; you must not give a daughter of yours to a son of theirs nor take a daughter of theirs for a son of yours, for this would turn away your children from following me to serving others gods" (Deuteronomy 7:3–4). Those people lived in close proximity to the Israelites, and the possibility of assimilation to their culture was real. The term *Canaanite* applied to all seven nations living in the land of Canaan in close proximity to the Israelites. Other biblical prohibitions against mixed marriages directed against the Ammonites, Moabites, and Egyptians had to do with historical memories of antagonistic relationships and not the concern about absorption/assimilation. Intermarriages with non-Israelite individuals who came from other lands but lived in Canaan were not prohibited. For example, the Bible permits a soldier to marry his captive. Here, though, is described a separation ritual, for the captive woman had to shave her head, cut her nails, and for a month mourn her parents who were to be considered dead (Deuteronomy 21:10–14). As the noted biblical scholar Yehezkel Kaufmann points out,

> In biblical days the prohibition of mixed marriages was directed at specific nations, but otherwise intermarriage was permitted. Ammonites and Moabites are excluded for historical reasons (Deuteronomy 23:4). Egypt, on the other hand, is favored for historical reasons (Deuteronomy 23:8–9). . . . The sources speak continually of mixtures between Israel and the nations. . . . The rule was that the third generation [of Egyptians and Edomites] who settled in Israel was permitted to join the community of "YAHWEH" and was considered Israelite (Deuteronomy 23:8) (1960, p. 308).

There is no term for proselyte (convert) in the Bible. The original denotation of *ger* in the Bible means simply a stranger. The identification of the term *ger* (*gioret*, the feminine term) as proselyte is found much later in rabbinic, medieval, and modern literature.

The non-Israelite, the *ger*, who married an Israelite was evidently not asked to go through a conversion ceremony as an abandonment of one faith or people in favor of another faith or way of life. The Bible indicates a naturalization process was accepted rather than a specific symbolic act of commitment to a faith. The concept of *ger* is treated twenty-seven times in the Pentateuch and nowhere is an obstacle placed on a *ger* marrying an Israelite. The underlying rule is "one law to the stranger and homeborn in your midst" (Numbers 15:15). There are a few distinctions between a *ger* and a homeborn, but marriage was not one of them. The main differences were religious, relating to sacrifical acts for the *ger*. For example, the *ger* was not obligated to follow the dietary laws and, thus, a nonkosher animal or carcass could be sold to him or her. In addition, during the Commonwealth period, the *ger* could not become king, very much like the provision of the Constitution of the United States that the office of president is to be filled by a native born citizen. Otherwise impediments were not placed upon a *ger*. He or she was permitted to marry an Israelite.

Historical research of that period also has not produced definitive evidence that circumcision of the male, a time-hallowed practice among Jews dating back to the time of Abraham and universally practiced today, was required of the *ger* who married a Jew. Abraham was commanded: "When they are eight days old, all your male children must be circumcised, generation after generation of them, no matter whether they be born within your household or bought with your money" (Genesis 17:2–13). This command would logically imply that in joining a Jewish household a non-Israelite would be required to undergo circumcision. However, it can also be maintained that the term "bought with your money" is directed specifically to servants who were considered the property of their masters and, hence, the covenantal requirements including circumcision also applied to them. Likewise, circumcision is mentioned for a *ger* living in Canaan who wished to partake of the Paschal sacrifice. The eating of such a sacrifice is also indicative of a covenantal relationship between the Jewish people and God. To enter into the covenant, one had to be fully Jewish, and circumcision was mandated. But nowhere, except for the aforementioned covenantal reasons, is circumcision mandated. In that period marriage was not a covenantal rite. Here may be our first indication of the separation of religious from ethnic-kin roles. Higher standards apply for full religious participation than for mere family relationships.

The biblical incident of Dinah and Shechem does not refute the above statement. Dinah was violated by Shechem, the son of Hamor (Genesis 34:1–31). Shechem, a heathen, then wished to marry the daughter of Jacob whom he had raped. He is advised by Jacob's sons that he and his entire tribe would have to undergo circumcision. The biblical text suggests that this ad hoc requirement was made due to the concern of Jacob's family over Shechem's father's invitation to assimilate: "Intermarry with us; give your daughters to us, take our daughters for yourselves, *and you will dwell among us*" (our emphasis) (Genesis 34:9). It seems from the text that the situation was a case of a Jewish family in danger of being assimilated by the dominant population; they were a small familial group surrounded by large powerful tribes. Therefore, a strict requirement was added for intermarriage.[2]

As the tribes gradually settled down in the land, they found themselves frequently involved in battles with neighboring kingdoms. Initially, the were satisfied to have temporary military and organizational leadership provided by so-called judges, with priests providing religious leadership. Eventually, though, they felt the

---

2. The subsequent killing of the Shechemites after the circumcisions raises some doubt as to whether the circumcisions were requested to facilitate intermarriage, to dissuade Shechem because of the serious requirement, or to weaken the Shechemites so they could more easily be slaughtered.

need for a more centralized ruling structure, and against the wishes
of God as conveyed by Samuel, a prophet-priest, demanded a king.
With the crowning of Saul, the first Jewish Commonwealth was
established about 1000 BCE.[3] As a sovereign people, the Israelites'
fear of foreign influences was lessened and a hospitable attitude
toward marriage with the stranger emerged. King Solomon, in order
to forge alliances with the surrounding people, married many gentile wives, and not even the voices of the prophets were raised
against him. For the next 600 years, the prophets warned against
worship of foreign gods but did not call for a ban on intermarriage.
In 722 BCE, when the northern ten tribes were taken captive by the
Assyrians, prophets in the remaining kingdom of Judea continually
warned against social injustice and falling away from God's laws but
did not add restrictions to the role of the *ger*. This lenient state of
affairs lasted until the destruction of the First Commonwealth by
the Babylonians in 586 BCE.

In sum, in this postpatriarchal period when the Israelites were in
control of their land and had their own government, they were
allowed to intermarry with any but their historical enemies without
restrictions. Apparently, the Israelites were sufficiently confident
that the stranger would be integrated into the dominant life of the
people and believed that the danger of their sons and daughters
following the way of the heathens because of intermarriage was
nonexistent.

The rite of circumcision is not mentioned in the Bible as a
requirement for marriage. To be sure, it may also be argued that
the rite was such a hallowed practice that silence may suggest that
it was taken for granted that a *ger* underwent circumcision if he
married a Jew. However, it can be stated with a degree of certainty
that no formal ceremony of conversion was mandated in that phase
of Jewish history.

Thus, we see that the patriarchal period and the early Israelite
period illustrate that when the faith of the community is threatened
by outside forces, severe restrictions are placed on intermarriage,
and when the community sees no threat, intermarriage restrictions
are not promulgated. During those periods, there were no standardized procedures for conversion rites, since one was accepted into the
Jewish community through association and not conversion. No term

---

3. BCE is the scholarly and Jewish designation, Before the Common Era, for the
time period some Christians call BC.

for proselyte is found in the Bible, and circumcision is mandated for full religious participation but not for marriage. The distinction of circumcision for religious but not for marital participation marks the beginning of separation of ethnic from religious concerns, which had not been distinguished in the patriarchial period.

End of the Biblical Period

At the close of the First Commonwealth when the Temple was destroyed in 586 BCE by the Babylonian Empire, the open attitude toward the stranger that prevailed in the postpatriarchal times was no longer acceptable to all authorities. With the loss of Jewish sovereignty and a large segment of the people in captivity, mixed marriages became a major concern. "Who would absorb/assimilate whom" was back on the Jewish agenda. In 536 BCE, Ezra and Nehemiah were authorized by Cyrus the Great of Persia, who had defeated the Babylonians, to rebuild the Temple and to establish a second Jewish Commonwealth. When those leaders returned from exile they found chaotic conditions in Jerusalem. The local population was depleted and demoralized. The historian Salo Baron estimates that "fully a third of the pre-war population of Judea was forcibly removed by the conqueror; the Jews, bereft of leadership, began to intermarry in great numbers and the popular religion of Canaan asserted itself" (1952, p. 85). Those intermarriages resulted in the emergence of a group of people known as the Samaritans. They consisted of foreign colonists and the descendents of the Israelites who escaped the destruction of the Northern Kingdom of Israel at the hands of the Assyrians in 722 BCE. Their religion was a mixture of Judaism and idolatry. When the Samaritans offered assistance in rebuilding the Temple, Ezra and Nehemiah feared their influence on the returnees and, also fearing that the future survival of Judaism was at stake, took drastic measures in order to eliminate alien influences. Ezra and Nehemiah proscribed marriages with the Samaritans. "We will not give our daughters to the peoples of the land or take their daughters for our sons" (Nehemiah 10:30). In the book of Ezra, we find an even harsher statement. In the renewal of the covenant between the people of Israel and God, Ezra insisted that the men who had intermarried had to break up their marriages and families. "Now, therefore let us make a covenant with our God to put away all foreign wives and the children born to them" (Ezra 10:3). Marriage was no longer to be viewed as a personal arrangement between families but was to be part of a covental (religious) relationship with God and, therefore, subject to strict controls.

The self-confident attitude toward the *ger* that we find during the First Commonwealth abated during the days of the second Temple, 536 BCE to 70 CE. Throughout most of the period of the Second Commonwealth, Israel was subservient to foreign rulers and never recovered the sense of confidence that marked its predecessor, the kingdom established by the House of David. The fear of being assimilated that prevailed in Judea because of its internal weakness was also due to the changed position of the Jew in the ancient world. Judea was no longer the only center of Jewish life. The Jews who returned with Ezra and Nehemiah to the land of Judea were impoverished while the most affluent ones continued to live in Babylonia and developed a creative community. As Persia gave way to Greece and the armies of Alexander the Great conquered the Near East, new opportunities for commerce developed. Jewish merchants began to travel great distances, and those who settled outside of Judea formed substantial diasporas. Centers of Jewish life sprang up in Egypt, Rome, Syria, and other far-flung communities. Jews interacted with gentiles, and both exerted influences on each other. Many Jews were attracted to Hellenism, and many gentiles were attracted to Judaism, which up to that time had been relatively unknown outside of Judea. The danger of foreign influences became more acute, and a serious concern about marriage outside the faith and people followed. Consequently, the beginning of formal conversion to Judaism emerged, leading to the requirement of circumcision for males.[4]

A famous case of circumcision for the purpose of conversion is recorded in the writings of Josephus, a Jewish historian in the period of the Second Commonwealth. Josephus relates the story of the conversion of Queen Helena and her son, Izates of Adiabene, a kingdom in the upper Tigris region. Helena converted first. Following the queen's conversion, her son, Izates, who came under the influence of a Jewish merchant, Ananias, decided to follow his mother's example. When Eleazar, a Galilean Jew, heard about the conversion, he urged Izates to undergo circumcision despite the fact

---

4. We are aware of the forced Idomite conversions during the period of the Maccabees; however, many scholars maintain that those conversions were for political rather than religious or ethnic reasons. Therefore, we have not used this event as an example.

that Helena and Ananias did not consider it necessary to do so. Eleazar, however, was insistent. His plea was that the lack of circumcision would be "the greatest offense against the law and thereby against God" (*Antiquties* 20:34 ff).

The Adiabene tale is an important illustration of a community increasingly becoming wary about those eager to join it. On one hand, the fact that others wished to join the Jewish ranks was a source of satisfaction to the Jew; but, on the other hand, there were those who were concerned lest a large number of joiners would lead to increased foreign influences and a distortion of historic Judaism. One way to resolve the issue was to insist on stringent requirements for admission into the fold. The biblical concept of the *ger,* the stranger living in the land of Israel, was now broadened to include the one who is a *ger,* a stranger who never set foot in Judea. For that *ger* the requirement of circumcision was called for by some of the rabbis. We also find that at the end of the Second Commonwealth, new terms were used in addition to that of *ger.* In the late books of the Bible (see, for example, Esther 8:1), we find the word *mityahadim,* gentiles becoming Jewish. In Malachai, another late book in the Bible, a gentile who accepted part but not the totality of Judaism was no longer called a *ger* but a "fearer of the Lord."

Throughout the Second Commonwealth period, there was an ambivalence in the approach to gentiles who wished to join the Jewish people. While Ezra and Nehemiah, as previously stated, were exclusionary in their approach, there were others at that time who were concerned that exclusion would lead to the insulation of the Jewish community. Thus, the book of Ruth, which according to many modern Bible scholars originated during the period, is understood as a polemic against the ban on intermarriage issued by Ezra and Nehemiah. Ruth, in addition to being a gentile, is also a Moabite whom Scripture categorically prohibits from entering *Khal Adonai,* the congregation of Israel, until the tenth generation. The widow Ruth, who had lived with her Jewish husband outside the land of Israel, clings to her mother-in-law, Naomi, and pleads to be allowed to return with Naomi to the land of Israel. Ruth's words to Naomi, "Entreat me not to leave you and to return from following after you; for where you go I will go, where you lodge I will lodge, your people will be my people, and your God my God" (Ruth 1:16), have become symbolic of proselytes who accept Judaism enthusiastically. Ruth follows Naomi back to the land of Israel, marries a Jewish man, and, tradition has it, became the great-grandmother of the revered King

David. No conversion ceremony is recorded for Ruth. Ruth is the Jew by choice par excellence. It is only at a later date, as we shall see, that the rabbis interpreted the story of Ruth in such a manner that Ruth's words become criteria for conversion.

The author of Ruth, obviously, welcomed the gentile and, if it is a polemic against Ezra and Nehemiah, as many scholars believe, the book's message is that in the land of Israel the gentile will eventually be absorbed and, therefore, mixed marriages pose no threat to the community.

In summary, we see that the exile in 586 BCE shook the confidence of the Jews in their ability to survive on the basis of nationalism alone. Ezra and Nehemiah, architects of the Second Commonwealth, upon their return from Babylonian exile feared the syncretization of the Jewish faith taking place in the land of Israel and the influences emanating from the growing diasporas. They demanded of Jews purity of faith and required that marriages be consecrated only between born Jews. The Second Commonwealth that they established never had the same measure of sovereignty as the First Commonwealth. At its inception it was ruled by the Persian Empire, later the Jews became dependent on the good will of Alexander the Great, and during the Maccabean era, Hellenism, the Greek influence on the ancient world, weakened the loyalty of the Jewish community toward their ancestral faith. In the latter part of the biblical period, in contrast to its earlier period, the convenantal aspects of Judaism rather than its familial or national aspects begin to emerge. The book of Ruth is probably a polemic against this trend.

To review the information about proselytes for the entire biblical period, three attitudes can be discerned. In the patriarchal tales we are told of a small familial group dedicated to monotheism, determined to transmit their religion to their children. Fearful of outside influences, they hoped that their children would marry only within their extended family, live close to them, and be influenced by their example. Marriages with nearby strangers were discouraged. As the family tribes increased, they forged themselves into a kingdom, with a land of their own, being ruled by judges and then by kings and having a central religious sanctuary. As a sovereign people, they were unafraid to marry a stranger living in their midst who accepted monotheism. They were confident that the *ger* would eventually be absorbed into the life of the people. In the latter part of the biblical period, which was a time of turmoil for the Commonwealth with its future threatened by powerful empires, the religious leadership began to emphasize the covenantal aspects of the religion and demand a purity of faith in order to stave off religious syncretism.

TALMUDIC PERIOD

Problems for the Jewish people intensified with the destruction of the second Temple in the year 70 CE by the Romans and the crushing defeat of the Bar Kochba rebellion in 135 CE, which put an end to the Jewish Commonwealth. The land and the temple that united the people in the past were gone and could no longer serve as a unifying force. Jews who lived in the various diasporas such as Babylonia, Egypt, or Rome continued to be exposed to foreign social and intellectual ideas by their neighbors. In addition, Christianity, which also professed monotheism, was becoming a power. The Talmud, a unique work containing discussions among the rabbis over a period of six centuries, 100 BCE to 500 CE, dealt with these enormous problems. The discussions gave rise to what is known today as rabbinic Judaism. The Talmud is the authoritative guide even today and is important for our discussion of proselytism. In the Talmud, rabbis charted a new course for the entrance of a gentile into the Jewish community. These events affected attitudes toward proselytism. The Talmud no longer defined a *ger* as one who lived in a sovereign Jewish state who could be absorbed in the community but as one who enters into a covenantal community. The *ger,* having no option for citizenship, had to undergo a formal conversion ritual that initiated him or her into a religious covenantal community. The proselyte was required to appear before three Jews who constitute a *bet din,* a court of Jewish law, and they were to address him or her as follows:

> "What reason have you for desiring to become a proselyte; do you not know that Israel at the present time is persecuted and oppressed, despised, harassed, and overcome by affliction?" If he replies, "I know and yet am unworthy," he is accepted forthwith and is given instruction in some minor and major commandments (*Yebamot* 24b).

The male proselyte is to undergo circumcision and both the female and the male are required to immerse themselves in a *mikvah,* a ritual bath. In making religious decisions, the rabbis try to find rationale in the biblical texts for their innovations; therefore, they found precedents for formal conversion in the Torah. Since the first Jew, Abraham, underwent circumcision as a sign of a *brit*, a covenant, the proselyte, in rabbinic teaching, likewise is "a new born babe" and through circumcision becomes the spiritual child of Abraham to be absorbed into the covenantal community founded by the patriarch.

In addition, the immersion of proselytes in water is also a covenantal rite derived from a biblical interpretation of Israel's covenant with God at Mount Sinai. They were commanded through Moses, "go to the people, sanctify them today and tomorrow, and let them wash their garments" (Exodus 19:10). The rabbis adduce from these biblical verses that if one was to wash one's garments for sanctification, surely one was to wash oneself. (See commentary on the verse by Hertz, 1938, p. 292.) And since the covenant of the past represented a change of status, a cleansing of oneself from past beliefs, and a new start, the proselyte now also had to undergo these rituals.

The conversion ceremony represents a new mind-set toward the gentile world. One could no longer be naturally absorbed within the community. A proselyte had to undergo religious ritual requirements if he or she wished to be a Jew and could no longer marry a Jew unless all the requirements for conversion were first met. A conversion ritual constituted a radical departure from biblical days when a *ger* living in Judea was required only to observe ethical principles known as the seven Noahide laws. The *ger* in the Talmud is required to observe all the commandments even as a born Jewish son or daughter is commanded. The biblical concept of *ger* as a resident alien ceases to exist in the Talmudic era and is replaced by the concept of the *ger tzedek*, the righteous proselyte.

As a result of these strict requirements there arose the problem of large numbers of gentiles who were attracted to Judaism but who were not ready to fulfill the ritual requirements imposed by the religious authorities. Their absorption into the Jewish community was vigorously debated. Could a covenantal community maintain its character if a large number of would-be proselytes brought up with alien beliefs were absorbed, or would they eventually dilute the covenant? Some religious authorities maintained that proselytes and potential proselytes were not to be encouraged and that the rules of admission should be stringent, while others wished to remove as many obstacles as possible, maintaining that Judaism is a universal religion and gentiles should be encouraged to come "under the wings of God." The debate was not a theoretical discussion for Jewish learning but had immediate ramifications. The historian Josephus (38–100 CE), who lived during the time of the collapse of the Jewish state and the ascendancy of the diaspora, described the vast appeal that Judaism had for the gentile:

> The masses have long since shown a keen desire to adopt our religious observances, and there is not one city, Greek or barbarian, nor a single nation to which our custom of abstaining from work on the seventh day has not spread and where fasts and the lighting of lamps and many other prohibitions in matter of food is not observed (as cited by Baron, 1952, pp. 173–174).

What was to be the attitude toward those who adhered to many Jewish practices but had reservations about a total acceptance of the covenantal requirements? Were they to be treated as outsiders or were they to be accepted in some form? Should Jews maintain a mission to the outside world? These were some of the questions that agitated rabbinic thought. There is no definitive evidence in Jewish sources that Jews engaged in missionary activities as the Christian New Testament claims, "Woe to you, scribes and Pharisees, you hypocrites for you travel over sea and land to make one proselyte and, when you have him, you make him twice as fit for hell as you are" (Matthew 23:15). However, missionizing can be accomplished by exemplary living, and Jews who settled in all parts of the ancient world practicing Judaism drew many gentiles to their belief by example. George Foote Moore, in his monumental work *Judaism in the First Centuries of the Christian Era,* writes,

> The belief in the future universality of the true religion . . . led to efforts to convert the gentiles to worship the one true God . . . and made Judaism the first missionary religion of the Mediterranean world. . . . The phrase must, however, be understood with a difference. The Jews did not send out missionaries . . . to proselytize among the heathen. They were themselves settled by the thousands in all the great centers and in innumerable smaller cities. . . . Their religious influences were exerted chiefly through synagogues . . . which were open to all whom interest and curiosity drew to their service (1927, pp. 323–326).

The talmudic passages bearing on proselytism seem to confirm the fact that the rabbis were keen on spreading their faith to the gentile communities, and many spoke with great enthusiasm regarding converts. Not only were they open to proselytism, but some would accept proselytes without any prior condition. Passages in the Talmud, particularly statements from Hillel the Elder (end of first century BCE to beginning of first century CE), illustrate this willingness to share Judaism with gentiles.

Hillel would accept proselytes who refused to adhere to rabbinic teaching by only accepting the written law, namely the Torah, but not the oral law. A native Jew who would utter such sentiments would have been labeled a heretic. Nevertheless, Hillel was favorably disposed to such proselytes. The Talmud records that a certain heathen once came before Shammai and asked him, "How many Torahs have you?"

> "Two," he replied, "the Written Torah and the Oral Torah."
> "I believe you with respect to the Written but not with respect to the Oral Torah. Make me a proselyte on condition that you teach me the Written Torah (only)."
> (But) he scolded him and repulsed him with anger. When he went before Hillel, he accepted him as a proselyte (*Shabbat* 31a).

The significance in this passage is that Hillel the Elder encouraged the heathen to join the covenantal community. Of course, the Talmud states that Hillel eventually convinced the proselyte to study and to accept the oral law as well, but the text also reveals the attitude of Hillel that initially it is incumbent on rabbis not to discourage gentiles who are exploring the possibility of joining the Jewish community. The same Hillel also would encourage a prospective proselyte to join the Jewish community even though he asked to be converted to Judaism for the sake of becoming a high priest (*Shabbat* 31a). To Hillel, conversion was the *beginning* of a relationship of Jewish religious practice, not the end.

Other authorities like Hillel wished to eliminate as many barriers as possible in order to encourage proselytism. Even as late as the second century CE, mandatory circumcision and use of the *mikvah* for converts became a subject of debate between Rabbi Eliezer and Rabbi Joshua. According to Rabbi Eliezer, if the candidate was circumcised but had not been immersed in the *mikvah* water, he was a "bona fide" proselyte. According to Rabbi Joshua, if he performed the proper immersion ablution but was not circumcised, he was a proper proselyte (*Yebamot* 46a). Each rabbi validated his statement with quotations from Scripture, but could we not speculate that, even as late as the second century, there were rabbis who maintained that neither circumcision nor immersion were the sine qua non for conversion? Is it possible to reason that there were rabbis who not only begrudgingly accepted converts but who encouraged proselytism by removing many of the ritualistic requirements that at times served as an impediment?

Scattered throughout the Talmud one finds an openness toward proselytism. "The Holy One, Blessed be He, exiled Israel among the nations only in order to increase proselytes" (*Pesachim* 87b). A benediction formulated in talmudic times that to this day is recited daily at services includes a prayer in praise of the proselyte. "Toward the righteous and pious, toward the elders of Thy people, the House of Israel, toward the proselytes of righteousness, and toward us also, may Thy tender mercies be stirred, O Lord our God" (*Tosefta Berakhot* 3:25). Rabbis taught that the proselyte should be fully accepted by Jews. "He who perverts justice against a proselyte is deemed as though he has turned against God Himself" (*Hagigah* 5a). No slur was permitted against a Jew whose parents were converts. "You must not reproach a descendent of proselytes with his former ancestry" (*Mishnah Baba Mezia* 4:10). Rabbi Simon b. Lakish, a third century Palestinian scholar, idealized the convert. "The proselyte is more beloved unto God than the multitudes at Sinai, for this one accepted the Kingdom of Heaven without rumble and thunder" (Braude, 1940, p. 25).

Talmudic legends abound with biblical personalities who obviously were gentiles, but in the legends they appear as proselytes. Conversion was ascribed to Bithia, the daughter of Pharaoh who saved Moses; Jethro, the father-in-law of Moses; and Rehab, who helped Joshua capture Jericho and who became an ancestor of the prophet Jeremiah (Braude, 1940, p. 36). In rabbinic tradition proselytes, or sons of proselytes, are some of the most distinguished rabbis; for example, Shemiah, the head of the Sanhedrin (Jewish supreme court) in the fifth century BCE and his colleague Avtalyon; Aquilla, the translator of the Bible into Greek; Rabbi Meir, whose legal opinions are said to be the basis for the *Mishnah;* and Rabbi Akiba, a scholar and martyred patriot of the second century CE (*Sanhedrin* 96b).

Laudatory statements and sentiments about converts were by no means unanimous. There were rabbis who questioned whether a powerless people suffering the loss of Jewish sovereignty could absorb gentiles in great numbers or whether Judaism would be syncretized by the gentile world unless it maintained its purity. The Talmud thus records both laudatory and unfriendly statements, but at no time is conversion ruled out. Often we read that the same rabbi who made an unfriendly statement acknowledged in another case that a true proselyte was to be accepted without any reservations. Thus, Rabbi Eliezer ben Hyrcanus who said, "It is because the proselyte's temper is bad that scripture warns him in many places" also said, "when a man comes to you wishing to convert to Judaism as long as he comes in the name of God, for the sake of heaven, do thou likewise befriend him and do not repel him" (*Mekhilta Amalek* 3, cited by Braude, 1940, p. 40). Rabbi Hiyya said, "Put no confidence in a proselyte until the twenty-fourth generation for he holds onto his leaven," yet the same Rabbi Hiyya said "when a proselyte accepts the yoke of heaven in love and fear and is converted for the sake of heaven . . . God loves the proselyte" (cited by Braude, 1940, p. 41).

No uniform attitude toward the convert is found in the period of the Talmud. The Talmud records a collection of individual opinions, some in praise of converts, others in judgment. We can only speculate that much had to do with the respective rabbi's experiences with gentiles. Rabbi Helbo, a third century rabbi who lived during a repressive period under the Roman Empire, probably expressed his opinion based on his personal experience when he said, "converts are as obnoxious to Israel as leprosy" (*Yebamot* 47:b). It is noteworthy that the commentary *Tosafot* (*Yebamot* 42b) considers this statement to be complementary because Rabbi Helbo also states, "converts are more careful regarding the commandments than other Jews, hence the difficulty Israel has in emulating them." On the other hand, Rav, who lived in the first century CE in Babylonia under peaceful conditions, gladly welcomed converts. "Whoever comes to be converted should be accepted. Do not inquire into motives of would-be converts. We may assume that they come for the sake of heaven."

The ambivalence in the talmudic period was resolved by establishing a uniform practice for conversion. If one wished to join the covenantal community, a male had to undergo circumcision and immersion and a female immersion. The convert was obligated to accept the teachings of *halachic* Judaism. A conversion ceremony was to take place in the presence of a *bet din,* a court of Jewish law consisting of three knowledgeable Jews. This format was accepted only after much debate.

Since the talmudic authorities authenticated their decrees by tracing their decisions to earlier sources, particularly the Bible, how were they now to justify the revered biblical personalities who married gentiles without any conversion, such as Joseph who married Asenath, an Egyptian daughter of a priest; Moses who married Zipporah, a daughter of a Midianite priest; and Boaz who married Ruth, a Moabite? The rabbis reinterpreted the ancient texts, reading into them the ceremony of conversion. One such example is in the interpretation given to the story of Ruth.

Kind David traced his ancestry to Ruth, yet we find no evidence of conversion of this Moabite woman in the book of Ruth. To the talmudic rabbis, this was unthinkable. Therefore, a legend based on the biblical story of Ruth was used to solve the dilemma for them.

According to the *Midrash,* since Ruth's decision to return to Israel could not be shaken, her mother-in-law, Naomi, in compliance with Jewish law that a prospective convert must at first be discouraged, warns her that Israelites must keep the Sabbath and feast days, to which Ruth answered, "where you go, I will go." (According to *Yebamot* 47a, the attention of the prospective convert must be directed to these ceremonial laws.) "Where you lodge, I will lodge" shows Ruth's acceptance of the restriction on a female being alone with a male who is not her husband. Naomi further says to Ruth, "We have one Torah, one God, one law, one command, the Eternal is one." Ruth answers, "Thy people shall be my people [accepting the 613 commandments incumbent on Jews] and thy God my God." "By whatever means you die, I will die" shows Ruth's understanding of the four forms of capital punishment used by the Jewish court—stoning, burning, decapitation, and strangulation. "And there I will be buried" demonstrates Ruth's acceptance of the rules of burial. "And she [Naomi] ceased speaking to her [Ruth]" indicates that Naomi's task was to present Ruth with some information on major laws and punishments, attempt to dissuade her from undertaking the obligations of a Jew, but not to overburden or cross-examine her too closely. When Ruth comes to Judea, despite her meeting the requirements for conversion, her brother-in-law refuses to marry her. According to the rabbinic interpretation of this story, which seems to sanction behavior that is against a direct biblical statement, Boaz was unaware that the law forbade only a Moabite *male* from entering *Khal Adonai;* a Moabite woman was permitted to do so. Becoming aware of the law, Boaz marries her (Ginzberg, 1941, pp. 32–34).

In summary, the talmudic period saw a restructuring of Judaism. The survival of the faith was threatened by the loss of statehood, dispersion, increased contacts with the gentile world, and the absence of a central authority. To fill the vacuum left by those developments, the emphasis shifted to a strengthening of the covenantal relationships between God and Israel. By entering that relationship, it was hoped that the proselyte would be able to overcome the pressures of the outside world and be totally absorbed into the Jewish community. A formal conversion procedure was designed to focus on that covenantal relationship. Thus, such requirements as circumcision, immersion in the *mikvah,* and acceptance of the commandments became part of normative Judaism. The *ger tzedek,* the righteous proselyte, meeting these requirements would in fact be a source of strength to the covenantal community.

The talmudic period also had to confront another challenge vis-à-vis the gentile world. Prior to the rise of Christianity, the issue seemed to have been how to insulate Judaism from outside influences and how to make certain that the convert knowlingly accepted the covenant between God and the Jewish people. With the rise of Christianity, new realities emerged that in fact if not in theory resulted in a moratorium on conversion to Judaism.

Much of the world population was ready for a change from pagan polytheism to ethical monotheism, but, whereas Judaism in the past attracted gentiles, now the new faith, Christianity, won the hearts and minds of the pagan world. The stringent talmudic requirements, particularly circumcision for conversion even for adult males, served as a source of discouragement. The gentile could now choose Christianity with fewer religious requirements as the road to monotheism, and the popularity of Judaism began to diminish. Paul found a ready-made audience for his missionary work. The book of Acts describes Paul as preaching in the synagogue of Antioch "to Jews and you that fear God." The message inspired gentiles more than those who were born Jews. Paul is portrayed as being annoyed with the Jews who doubted his message. "It was necessary that the word of God should first have been spoken to you [Jews], but since you put it from you and judge yourself unworthy of everlasting life, we turn to the gentiles" (Acts 13:46). His message was directed to gentiles who could now leave their former faith. Without accepting Judaism, they could transfer from paganism to Christianity. In addition, circumcision that was required by talmudic law was not mandated by Christianity. "In Christ Jesus neither circumcision nor uncircumcision is of any avail but [only] faith working through love" (Galatians 5:16). The gentile seeking a new faith, attending the synagogue, being attracted to Judaism, but not being fully converted heard a new message that offered monotheism without the strictness of the talmudic laws.

POST–TALMUDIC PERIOD

As Christianity established itself in the world, the number of conversions to Judaism was greatly limited. Not only because Christianity won the hearts and minds of the pagan world, but also because in the fourth century CE, when Christianity became the official faith of the Roman Empire, conversion to Judaism was forbidden on pain of death. That edict for capital punishment promulgated in 315 CE was later expanded in 403 CE to apply not only to the Christian convert but also to members of the Jewish court who accepted a gentile as a convert. As a result, from the days of Constantine until the breaching of the ghetto walls at the end of the eighteenth century, proselytism to Judaism became a rare phenomenon.

It is noteworthy that even in the early Christian period when the transfer from one religion to another was considered a capital offense, there were courageous souls who joined the Jewish community and managed to find an equally courageous accepting *bet din*. The proselyte fearing for his life had to hide and to roam from one country to another as a fugitive from "justice." This was the fate of the Archibishop Andreas, chief priest of the province of Bari (now in southeast Italy), who had to flee to Egypt to save himself. In 1102 a Norman proselyte, Obadiah, a first-year student in the priesthood greatly influenced by Andreas, wrote pamphlets calling upon Christians to return to the religion of Israel, and, after the Christian authorities imprisoned him, he succeeded in escaping to Baghdad. Obadiah visited Jewish communities in Syria, Palestine, and Egypt, was befriended by the head of the Baghdad academy, and lived in his home for some time (*Encyclopedia Judaica*, 1977, p. 1187).

One should not think that the former Archbishop Andreas and Norman, the proselyte, found a haven in the Moslem part of the world because Moslems were more tolerant of proselytism than Christians; they were not. Christian converts to Judaism were safe in Islamic countries because it was not against the Islamic faith for a Christian to become a Jew; however, Islam forbade conversion from Islam either to Judaism or to Christianity. A series of discriminatory regulations were promulgated during the Caliphate of Omar (634–644 CE) making pariahs of Jews and Christians. Moslems were bidden to convert non-Moslems but did not object if Jews converted Christians to Judaism.

That proselytism occurred in the Middle Ages we see from the writings of Judah Halevi (1086–1145 CE). The historian Graetz (1949) reflected the esteem that Jews bore Halevi: "to describe him fully, one would have to borrow from poetry and her richest colors and her sweetest song." One of the greatest philosophical Jewish writings, known as the *Sefer-ha-Kuzari,* written by Judah Halevi, is based on an episode in Jewish history in the year 740 CE. It describes the conversion of the Khazars, a Tartar nation located on the western banks of the Caspian Sea between the Don and the Volga.

A dialogue takes place in which a Christian, a Moslem, an Aristotelian, and a Jew appear before Budan, king of the Khazars. The king listens to the arguments presented but is particularly impressed with the Jewish representative Hver as he expounds from Judaism on philosophy, liturgy, history, and concepts of God, Messiah, and the Holy Land. When the Khazar monarch alludes to the degraded condition of the Jew, Hver rejoins,

> Do not believe that I, though agreeing with thee, admit that we are dead. We still hold connection with the Divine influence through the laws which He has placed in us as a link between us and Him. . . . We are not like the dead but rather like a sick and attenuated person who has been given up by the physicians, but yet hopes for a miracle or an extraordinary recovery (Minkin, 1963, p. 124).

The king accepts the Jewish religion both for himself and for his people. The Jewish kingdom lasted until 969 CE when it suffered its ultimate defeat by the Duke of Kiev.

The tale of the conversion of the Khazars is significant for our study on two counts. First, the setting is in a land that was free from Christian and Moslem intolerance. In the absence of pressure from Christianity and Islam, Judaism had an opportunity to present its case and in a free contest could prevail. Second, the fact that in the Middle Ages Judah Halevi chose the episode of conversion of the Khazars as a vehicle for expounding Judaism shows that the biblical eschatological hope for the ultimate conversion of humanity to Judaism was still very much alive in the hearts of Jews. It is noteworthy that little is found in Jewish medieval writings about the Khazar kingdom even though the *Sefer-ha-Kuzari* was studied diligently as a philosophical text of Judaism. Could it be that living in Christian or Moslem lands, Jews avoided that part of their history for fear that the tale about conversion to Judaism would not be looked upon with favor by the governments of those countries?

Another medieval figure, Maimonides (1135–1204 CE), widely described as the greatest rabbi since the days of Moses, likewise left no doubt about his attitude toward proselytism. Obadiah, a convert to Judaism, addressed a question to Maimonides. In the daily prayers a Jew recites "Our God and God of our Fathers." Since his ancestors were gentiles, Obadiah asked whether he could use that phrase. It also seems from the answer of Maimonides that the convert was not fully accepted as a Jew by some members of the Jewish community. Maimonides defends Obadiah and addresses him in a most respectful manner as follows: "Master and teacher, the intelligent and enlightened Obadiah, the righteous proselyte. . . . You are a great scholar and possess an understanding mind, for you have understood the issues and know the right way." Maimonides urges him to say in the prayers "Our God and God of our Fathers," because the proselyte "is a pupil of our father Abraham and all proselytes are members of his household. . . . Further, do not belittle your lineage, if we trace our descent to Abraham, Isaac, and Jacob, your connection is with Him by whose world the universe came into being." Maimonides also assures him, "A man who left his father and his mother and birthplace and the realm of his people at a time when they are powerful, who understood with his insight, and who attached himself to this nation which today is a despised people, the slaves of rulers, and recognized and knew that their religion is true and righteous . . . the Lord does not call you a fool, but intelligent and understanding, wise and walking correctly, a pupil of Abraham our Father" (*Encyclopedia Judaica*, 1977, pp. 1188–1189).

Not all were as generous in their attitude toward proselytes as was Maimonides. During the Middle Ages that brought on the Crusades, the pogroms, and the ghettos, Jewish distrust and fear of the outside world were intensified. Jews as a persecuted group developed a mystical definition of themselves as distinct from other peoples. Rabbi Judah Loew (1530–1609 CE), known as Maharal of Prague, was a leading spokesman. He postulated that "there is a metaphysical difference between Jew and gentile." According to Rabbi Loew, each people has an essence peculiar to itself. That essence and form expresses itself in a specific people's particular language, dress, food, and geography. A person cannot change his or her essence nor can he or she relinquish it voluntarily or even under duress. It is not a matter of choice for the person to make. What is true of an individual is also true of a group as a whole; an Israelite in relation to a gentile occupies a different dimension of existence.

Rabbi Loew's argument leads to a logical conclusion that no conversion could ever take place, but even Rabbi Loew left the door open to proselytes. He justified their acceptance into the Jewish community with the argument that a proselyte who, in spite of the hostile environment, seeks Judaism demonstrates a prior and an innate disposition toward Judaism. Therefore, that individual was never anything but Jewish. "Do not ask," he says, "how can a proselyte accept the Torah? Has he not an inadequate spiritual disposition? There is no difficulty at all. The fact is that he wishes to share the fate of Jews, and he converts, so he is absorbed into the people of Israel and acquires [all] its spiritual characteristics" (Sherwin, 1982, p. 103). In essence what Rabbi Loew conveys is that the Jewish people is a clearly defined and perfect entity, and thus additions could disturb that perfection. But even he acknowledged that a sincere proselyte does not disturb that perfection. Rabbi Loew maintains that the new Jew is not really a convert but in reality a Jew from his or her day of birth.

To the nonmystic, the position of Rabbi Loew may seem farfetched, but those who instruct proselytes or who come in contact with them do not dismiss that position lightly. Proselytes often volunteer an explanation for their conversion: "Ever since I remember I felt as if I were a Jew." Many search their family tree diligently hoping to discover a Jewish ancestor. Maimonides, the rationalist, and Loew, the mystic, seem to be on the opposite side of the spectrum. The former accepts the convert as long as all conversion requirements are met, while the latter apparently discourages proselytism. Yet both are in agreement that Judaism mandates the acceptance of true proselytes.

The personal identification of a sincere convert, as well as the dire dangers resulting from conversion to Judaism that lasted until modern times, can be encapsulated in the case of the Polish count Valentine Potocki, who lived in the last part of the eighteenth century. The Polish authorities were informed that the count had become a Jew. Potocki was burned at the stake, but not before he recited the prayer found in the daily morning service, "Blessed be You our Lord . . . who sanctifies your name before multitudes" (*Encyclopedia Judaica*, 1977, pp. 934–935). One of the legends about Count Potocki is that a priest came to his cell to plead with him to recant and save his soul from damnation. Potocki refused on the basis of his understanding of the revelation at Sinai. He explained to the priest that the Israelites made a solemn pledge at Sinai, "we shall hearken, and we shall do," and that there is also a tradition that prior to the Sinai event God offered the Torah to the other nations who refused the offer. Potocki reasoned that not all Jews accepted the Torah and similarly not all gentiles refused the offer. He considered himself to be one of the few gentiles whose soul made the pledge to God that he accepted the Torah; hence, "how can I recant such a pledge".

Why is there so much discussion about proselytism in the post-talmudic period despite the very few cases of conversion to Judaism? One could speculate that even in the darkest days of persecution against Jews, particularly during the Crusader period when hundreds of Jewish communities were destroyed, the eschatological hope that the world will embrace the God of Israel was not dimmed. Judaism as a universal faith was proclaimed by Jews three times a day.

That theological concept is contained in the prayer *Aleinu L'Shabbeach*—it is our duty to praise (the Lord of all things). The first paragraph emphasizes that Israel is God's chosen people; the second paragraph calls for a united humankind under the Kingship of the Almighty. The prayer, originally composed by a third-century Rabbi Rav, was recited only on the Jewish New Year, but in the twelfth century during the time of the Crusades it was included in all services where it continues to be recited three times daily. The two paragraphs in juxtaposition are a powerful theological statement. The Jew sees him- or herself as having a purer and more religious life than others ("He made our lot unlike that of other people," Harlow, 1985, p. 161) and, at the same time, proclaims that in a future sanctified world, the Jewish community will be open to all

("May everyone accept the rule of your Kingship," Harlow, 1985, p. 161).

Thus, it appears that when both the proselyte and the proselytizer were in danger of death, proselytism was discouraged. That fear is expressed by Solomon Luria, a contemporary of Rabbi Loew. "Now that we are in a country not our own . . . should one of Israel accept a convert, he is a rebel and is responsible for his own death. . . . Hence, I give warning that anyone who is a participant in such acceptance today, when the gentile kingdom is stringent in its attitude, let his blood be on his own head" (Katz, 1961, p. 145).

A strong statement, but, if one reads between the lines, if the Christian world would relent in the persecution of the proselyte and proselytizer, even Solomon Luria would open the doors of Judaism to the righteous proselyte.

In conclusion, it is evident that proselytism never ceased in Jewish life even during the centuries of the domination of the Christian church from Constantine in 315 CE until the French Revolution in 1789. Records of individual heroism both for the proselyte and the proselytizer are to be found during that period. The often stated current opinions that Judaism opposes proselytism may be the result of the understandable hesitation that for centuries the Jewish community has displayed toward the would-be converts because of the probability of tragic retaliation by the Christian authorities. The discouragement was not rooted in theology but in fear of political consequences.

MODERN PERIOD

Until the end of the eighteenth century, rabbinic discussions on conversions to Judaism were mostly theoretical in nature. Proselytism was proscribed by church law, and social contacts between Jews and gentiles were almost nonexistent. Jews lived behind ghetto walls and developed a self-contained community. Centuries of discrimination and ghettoization had led to a Jewish existence that was distinct from surrounding gentile cultures and had turned inward in its concerns. Customs, beliefs, and life-styles had been codified and enacted with fairly narrow standards. Although there were variations for some customs (Ashkenazi and Sephardi, for example), individuals generally followed the local form without reference to other variations. Jewish males, excluded from the education, thought, and life-styles that were part of the gentile married Jews, though less difference in beliefs between converts and their Jewish partners.

First, in the general religious beliefs category, the ranking of beliefs is quite similar for all three groups. (See Table 4.5, Appendix.) Converts are more likely to view prayer as important than are either set of born Jews; converts and partners have more of a sense of the Divine presence in life than in-marrieds; in marrieds talk about religion more than partners or converts. Otherwise they are similar in their belief about God and the place of religion in their lives. The top three and bottom two ranked Jewish beliefs are shared by the three groups—top three: humans have free will, Judaism is more personally true, and there is only one God; bottom two: moral non-Jews will be saved, and God will send the Messiah. Otherwise there is considerable disagreement, especially between in-married Jews and converts. (Converts and partners tend to be similar in how strongly each belief is held.) Partners and converts are more concerned about beliefs than a moral life; converts have stronger beliefs in the convenantal relationship between God and Jews, the Bible as God's revealed word, the salvation of moral non-Jews, and the coming of the promised messiah. While rabbinic Judaism stresses the salvation of all non-Jews who follow the Noahide laws of basic morality, this belief is not shared by these religious Jews. It is not surprising that converts believe moral behavior to be sufficient since they are, by joining Judaism, rejecting the need for salvation through faith in Jesus.

As might be expected, converts hold more Christian beliefs than either set of Jews, although they are equally skeptical about the resurrection. Converts are slightly less likely than either group to believe that Jesus actually broke with Judaism, though all three groups rate this belief strongest. That may explain why they can feel positive about Jesus while still converting to Judaism. They view Jesus as a Jew and as their connector to Judaism. Christians who convert are not likely to see Jesus as do Jews in light of two thousand years of persecution in his name and are more likely to know him from the New Testament accounts that depict him as a persecuted Jew who tried to bring God's message to people. Converts are more likely to believe in his special role.

In the area of ethnic beliefs there is almost a reversal, with converts supporting concerns about the survival of Jews and Judaism that are not the highest concern for Jews. Converts seem most concerned with items that directly affect them—anti-Semitism,

feeling comfortable among Jews—but less concerned about community survival issues—voting for pro-Israel political candidates, supporting Israel, and having Jewish children marry Jews.

A further question about the perception of Jewish beliefs is
possible using the student data. We asked students to estimate what
they felt most Jews would answer to the beliefs questions as well as
to indicate their own beliefs. The extent and accuracy of potential
converts' awareness of Jewish beliefs represents something of the
standard to which they believe they will be held. Readers comparing
Appendix Tables 4.5 and 4.6 will note some differences between
convert beliefs and student beliefs. Generally speaking, the students
have scores somewhat higher than converts on all measures. While
that difference makes sense for the Christian beliefs, since the
student group includes those who decide not to convert in favor of
retaining their Christian identity, the higher scores for Jewish
religious and ethnic beliefs among the students are harder to
explain. It is true, though, that even the converts tended to have
stronger beliefs in all these categories, except the ethnic one, than
did born Jews (including their partners).

Students' views about Jewish beliefs do not significantly change
as a result of the introduction course. While Jews stress practice
over belief, since potential converts tend to be Christians who give
more primacy to beliefs, perhaps more attention needs to be given
to belief issues for potential converts. The greatest belief discrepan-
cies are in converts holding more Christian beliefs and lower ethnic
beliefs than born Jews. Yet converts may misperceive Jewish beliefs,
as we shall see.

We identified significant differences in each of the belief categories between the students' perception of Jewish beliefs, the reported
beliefs of their partners, and their own beliefs. We previously
learned that, generally speaking, partners' beliefs parallel both in-
married born Jews' and converts' beliefs, tending to fall midway
between them. Students tend to significantly underestimate the
general religious, Jewish religious, and ethnic beliefs of religiously
involved Jews. They are fairly accurate in their perception of the
minimal level of Christian beliefs held by Jews, but retain their own
more positive Christian beliefs.

Students believe themselves to be stronger adherents than Jews
to virtually all the beliefs. That misperception may inhibit their
community involvement, which is a less structured situation for
them than the practice of religious rituals. Thinking that Jews

aren't much concerned about ethnic issues and that they themselves are concerned more than most Jews puts potential and actual converts somewhat out of step with at least the religiously involved Jewish community, which strongly supports ethnic issues while being less concerned with religious beliefs. Also, while students recognize the importance to Jews of in-marriage, they retain a significantly lower concern about the matter.

Knowledge Variables

The ranking on the self-reported knowledge perception questions is fairly similar between the three groups. (See Table 4.7, Appendix.) Partners believe themselves less knowledgeable than in-married Jews while converts report more knowledge than either group. It should be remembered that these are self-evaluation questions rather than the results of objective tests. It is possible that Jews have a higher standard for what they consider good knowledge of Judaism because of their exposure to the breadth and depth of Jewish scholarship. On the other hand, it may be that converts, by studying purposefully as adults, indeed know more about Judaism than born Jews. Support for the first explanation, differences in standards, may be gotten from the fact that the converts scored higher than their partners on these items. Not only did the partners have a fairly good level of Jewish education, as we've already seen, but also most of them attended the same classes as the converts yet still rated their knowledge lower. By and large converts did not expend much studying time during or after this introductory course, so it is likely that they are misjudging the state of their knowledge. Some converts, no doubt, do go on to greater knowledge, but that is true of no more than a quarter of this group, as we've previously discussed. Since partners tend to rate themselves as less knowledgeable than in-married Jews even though they had more religious instruction and attended the classes, it may be that the introduction classes served to remind them of how little they knew when exposed to Jewish scholarship represented by the rabbis who taught the courses and by the course readings. Or it may be that they indeed lack knowledge as some commentators on intermarriage surmise. Still, it should be noted that all three groups tended to feel that they had fairly adequate knowledge about Jewish religious requirements.

In awareness of community resources, in-married Jews reported significantly better knowledge than either partners or converts. Since converts are likely to refer to their partners for information they need about resources, it is distressing to see that their partners know little more than they do.

Religious Practices

To what extent do the three grups differ in their religious practices? This is one critical concern in the debates about the role of converts that our previous chapter left unaddressed. Our data show that while there is fairly good agreement between the groups on the rank order of how frequently they engage in the various practices, both partners and converts tend to engage in less Jewish religious practice than religiously involved in-marrieds. (See Table 4.8, Appendix.) Some, but not all, of this difference comes from the fact that the out-marrieds tend to be Reform Jews while our in-married group is somewhat more Conservative. Generally, converts show even lower Jewish practices than their partners, especially for the more popular practices. Converts are more likely than their partners to have a menorah, observe Purim, refrain from Sabbath work, engage in study and prayer, eat kosher outside the home, and say the morning prayers. Unfortunately, our data do not support the observation that converts as a group are better at Jewish religious practices compared with our religious in-married Jews. (As we'll discuss shortly, they may be better when compared with the general Jewish community.) It may also be the case that a minority of converts are more committed and therefore more visible to rabbis. It is also true that our in-married born Jewish sample is somewhat older and thereby more traditional in their practice. Converts may look better when compared with born Jews of similar (younger) ages. In our study we can gauge this probability by comparing the converts with their partners who are similar in age. While there are not as many differences, out of this list of thirty-two practices converts match their partners on fourteen practices, exceed their partners on six practices, and fall short of their partners on twelve practices. This picture would not permit us to say that these converts as a group are "better Jews" than religiously oriented Jews as far as religious practices are concerned. Compared with their partners, these converts are more concerned about continuing to study Judaism, learning the prayers, and living near a synagogue. Whether there are resources to meet these concerns and, if met, whether convert practice would improve, we can only speculate. These responses do seem to indicate a need for accessible continuing education programs for converts. It should be noted that these converts completed their introductory studies before the addition of a basic Hebrew prayers program begun in 1988.

Both these partners and these converts engage in significantly more Christian practices than do in-married Jews, especially relating to Christmas presents and family gatherings. (See Table 4.9, Appendix.) This does not necessarily represent a serious threat to their own Jewish identity but may be a distraction for their children's identity.

Ethnic Involvements

Since the converts' contact with Christian practices is more ethnically (family) than religiously centered, we need to consider the extent of their ongoing involvements in the Jewish community as a potentially counterbalancing force. The top and bottom ranked involvements tend to be similar for all three groups. At the top, all three groups have Jewish art, watch Jewish-oriented TV programs or films, and subscribe to a Jewish newspaper or magazine; at the bottom, they tend not to belong to a Jewish community center or teach or organize Jewish classes or activities. (See Table 4.10, Appendix.) It is the Jewish partners in this case who tend to be the least involved of all three groups. Partners fall significantly behind in-married Jews on thirteen of the fifteen measures while converts fall short on only five measures; and on six measures converts exceed their partners. On balance, then, it seems that converts bring more positive Jewish ethnic involvements to their home life than a look just at their Christmas inputs would indicate, and they may indeed be helping to preserve a Jewish orientation to the household on an ongoing basis. However, they are less concerned about traditional ethnic involvements (Israel, living near Jews, and being near Jewish education) than are in-married Jews.

Children Socialization Plans

Our final major area of concern is the comparisons between the groups on their desire to involve their children Jewishly. Our data indicate that the ranking of concerns is similar between the groups; where there are differences, there is better rank agreement between partners and converts than either of those groups with in-married Jews. (See Table 4.11, Appendix.) However, the degree of concern about their children's Jewish identity and involvement is clearly different; partners and converts fall below born-Jews on the child Jewish involvement measures and above them on child Christian involvement and general choice measures. Partners and converts tend to agree more about the importance of Jewish religious practices for their children than about their ethnic involvements. In the latter case converts fall significantly below their partners in concern about their children's Jewish ethnic involvements. The largest areas of differences concern their children's friendship, dating, and marriage of Jews. We've already discussed this issue in Chapter 3.

COMPARISON OF OUR DATA WITH OTHER STUDIES

Practice Comparisons

Thus far, our comparison of converts with partners and with religiously involved, in-married born Jews would indicate that, as a group, converts are somewhat less involved or committed than Jews. But before we can draw our final conclusions about the contributions and fit of converts to the Jewish community as a whole, we need to know to what extent our born Jewish participants' behaviors are typical. For this we need to look at data from other studies that have incorporated a cross-section of born Jews, not just the religiously committed segment our data reflects. To anticipate our findings, converts' behaviors look much better when compared with Jewish community standards as a whole. The actual extent to which members of the Jewish community personally adhere to the practices advocated by the rabbis has only recently begun to be addressed. What do the data show?

As reported in a study of Jewish identity by Herman, the majority of U.S. Jews see Jews as both a religious group and a people (1977, p. 71), but their own attachment to Judaism as a religion is weak. For example, a Boston study reported by Sklare indicated that Jews attended religious services much less frequently than did the general U.S. population (1971, p. 118). The study found the following comparisons:

	Jews	Gentiles
Attended services more than once a month	17%	65%
Attend services monthly or so	21%	11%
Attend for main holiday only	39%	6%
Attend infrequently or never	23%	18%

Sklare indicated that, in general, Jews wanted their religion to:

1. Be defined in modern terms;
2. Require no social isolation or unique life-style;
3. Fit in with the holiday patterns of the dominant culture;
4. Be centered on child activities, and
5. Be performed annually or infrequently (1971, p. 114).

Generally, Jews wanted a Jewish education only to prepare their children for *bar/bat mitzvah* and confirmation. One study showed this trend by finding that 69.8 percent of eight- to twelve-year-old Jewish children were receiving instruction, but only 15.8 percent of thirteen- to seventeen-year-olds remained in Jewish-oriented programs. Jewish parents prefer a secular education for their children (only 13.4 percent were attending Hebrew day schools) with supplemental Jewish instruction either on Sundays (42.2 percent) or in an afternoon Hebrew school program (44.4 percent) involving a few hours a week only (Sklare, 1971, p. 173).

At the same time, even secular Jews maintain a high level of communal involvement. One study showed that 96 percent of Jews had only Jewish relatives, 77 percent had all their closest friends as Jews, 60 percent belonged to Jewish community organizations, virtually all of them gave to Jewish charities, and 90 percent felt a strong attachment to Israel (Waxman, 1983, p. 139). When asked, however, third generation Jews define themselves as a religious group in spite of their stronger ethnic-oriented practice (Friedman, 1986, pp. 34–37; Waxman, 1983, p. 81). Clearly, though, American Jews are increasingly secularized and interface during much of their educational and occupational life with the gentile world.

For comparing available data on born Jews and intermarrieds, Table 4.12 summarizes the findings of several recent major studies of Jews, including ours. As one can see, not every study provides comparable information. This is a common problem in social science research, but should not deter one from apprehending the general trends. We have chosen to compare the most frequently and consistently measured items.

Most studies provide information about observance of major Jewish religious holidays—Hanukah, Passover, Rosh Hashanah, and Yom Kippur. There is a high rate of observance of these holidays by religiously affiliated Jews and by converts (80 percent to 90 percent observe them), with substantially lower rates of observances by

TABLE 4.12
COMPARISON OF THE FORSTER-TABACHNIK DATA WITH OTHER STUDIES OF BORN JEWS AND INTERMARRIEDS

Variable*	General Communal Study Averages	Forster-Tabachnik Data				Mayer Data	
		Born Jews	Partners	Converts	Mixed	Converts	Mixed
Jewish Religious Practices							
Participate in a Passover seder	89%	96%	87%	93%	79%	95%	37%
Attend Yom Kippur services	86	93	81	87	48	88	20
Light Hanukah candles	84	90	94	86	63	92	33
Attend Rosh Hashanah services	84	91	80	82	46	88	21
Belong to a synagogue	49	99	64	69	29	87	NA
Attend Sabbath services	42	30	26	74	33	67	6
Fast on Yom Kippur	39	65	65	60	27	NA	NA
Light Sabbath candles	35	40	35	63	25	NA	NA
Keep kosher at home	24	21	12	14	11	NA	NA
Christian Religious Practices							
Attend a Christmas family gathering	13	13	56	58	95	65	95
Attend Easter family gatherings	NA	3	32	20	62	19	80
Jewish Ethnic Practices							
Subscribe to a Jewish newspaper	82	65	38	54	16	80	NA
Half or more friends as Jews	81	91	74	35	27	NA	NA
Important to support Israel	78	93	84	85	34	NA	NA
Give to Jewish charities	67	91	91	91	79	81	NA
Belong to a Jewish organization	37	60	27	38	9	67	NA
Plan to visit Israel	33	83	76	83	41	NA	NA

*Variables are listed within each category from highest to lowest according to the general communal study averages.

nonaffiliated Jews and mixed-married households (about one-third). Weekly Sabbath attendance is about 40 percent for Jews, but higher for conversionary households (about two-thirds). About one-third of Jews light Sabbath candles, while almost half of our converts do so. Two measures of personal life observances—using kosher meat and keeping separate dishes for meat and milk—rate a low 20 percent for affiliated Jews, about 10 percent for converts, and fewer than 5 percent for nonaffiliates. As for religious commitment, fewer than half of Jews but two-thirds of converts belong to a congregation. As might be expected, households with a member of Christian origin tend to participate in Christmas and Easter rituals two-thirds of convert households observe Christmas, 95 percent of mixed-marriage households), but 13 percent of fully Jewish households also observe Christmas. The usual observance tends to be having a Christmas tree, giving gifts, and participating in a family gathering (rather than in a religious service).

In sum, the available data show conversionary households participating in religiously oriented practices at a slightly higher rate than born Jews in general but somewhat less than the religiously involved Jews in our study. At the same time conversionary households have more Christian practices in place than in-married Jews as a whole.

Ethnic Comparisons

Community involvement tends to be through a network of Jewish friends. For Jews, membership is lower than is contribution to Jewish organizations. Only about a third read Jewish press materials, participate in adult Jewish education, or visit Israel. As far as the data show, convert participation in Jewish organizational life is about the same as that of Jews as a whole.

Information on Jewish items in the household from previous studies was available only for conversionary and mixed marriages. The data clearly indicate a substantial level of Jewish items present in conversionary households (ranging from a high of 93 percent for a menorah to a low of 18 percent for separate dishes) as compared with mixed marriages (56 percent with a menorah to 7 percent with separate dishes).

What about more active forms of ethnic involvement? Egon Mayer has found that as a whole, Jews by choice scored higher than born Jews on religious behaviors but lower on their attitudes about

Jewish identification (1983, p. 62). Our study supports this finding. His conclusion is instructive: "Jews by choice are probably more adept at acting like Jews in matters of religious practices than they are at feeling or thinking like Jews when it comes to social relationships" (Mayer, 1983, p. 63).

Sandberg suggests that ethnic identification should be subdivided into (1) cultural, which involves knowledge about Jewish History, thought, and issues and (2) national, which includes participation in Jewish organizational activites, giving to support Jewish activities, and concern with the continuation of the Jewish community. How do the intermarried fair in these areas?

Table 4.12 shows some data on these ethnic aspects. In the Mayer data, conversionary marriages have patterns similar to religiously oriented born Jews; mixed marriages are considerably lower. Our converts evidence lower ethnic involvement than the Mayer group. Unfortunately, many issues that are important in understanding the ethnic dimension have not been measured in other studies. Attitudes toward the Holocaust and anti-Semitism, preference for Jewish foods, liking of Jewish jokes, understanding common Yiddish terms, knowledge about and preference for Jewish community services, and so on have not been measured. Other areas such as concern for Israel, the importance of helping Jews, and the importance of Jewish survival have been found by Mayer to be strong among intermarrieds, but comparative data are not provided (1985, p. 110). Certainly mixed-marrieds show a markedly decreased commitment to the survival of the Jewish community in succeeding generations. Only 25 percent of them want their children to identify as Jews (Mayer, 1987; see our Table 3.16.) Since two-thirds of intermarriages are mixed marriages, the Jewish community has reason to be concerned. However, conversionary marriages clearly come closer to the Jewish norm.

While hard data are lacking, observers point to the difficulty gentiles have in the area of ethnic assimilation. Sklare concludes:

It is a sociological truth that although an individual may be converted to a faith he may remain outside of the group. The task of assimilating proselytes is relatively new for the Jewish community. . . . The born-Jew has a clear advantage over the convert through instrumentalities such as the nuclear family, the extended family and the all-Jewish clique group, he is provided with resources that help establish a Jewish community. The proselyte does not have such avenues—if his [sic] identity is to grow, it is strongly dependent upon his own desires as well as those of his spouse. But it can not flourish in a vacuum—it must be supported by a community that desires to include him (1971, p. 208).

Since gentiles are accustomed to defining a religious identity in terms of church attendance, it is not surprising that converts more readily and frequently attach themselves to synagogue membership and participation (a Boston study found 57 percent of Jews by choice belonged to and attended a synagogue versus 39 percent of born Jews) (Silberman, 1985, p. 315). However, it appears that converts need greater assistance in becoming part of the community of Jews. In principle, the 1965 *Rabbi's Manual* of the Rabbinical Assembly indicates that "it is highly desirable that [the applicant] be introduced to Jewish families in order to affect as pleasant and easy a transition period as possible into the Jewish faith and the Jewish community," but in practice, no formalized mechanism is in place to ensure that this occurs.

Several converts have spoken about the difficulties they face in being accepted by the Jewish people (Levin, 1986; Kukoff, 1981). Unlike Christians who open their arms and doors in great warmth, concern, and support for converts, Jews are generally suspicious, often evidencing the attitudes quoted by Elchhorn: "Anyone who wants to become a Jew must either be insincere or unbalanced" (1965). Jews by choice are surprised and hurt by evidence of nonacceptance from Jews that continues for years. No matter that at least some converts know more about Judaism, participate in synagogue services more devotedly, and are more likely to continue their studies than most born Jews. After facing the fears and rejections of Christian friends, dealing with their own doubts, and making sincere efforts and commitments to Judalism and to being a Jew, the struggle that converts face in gaining full acceptance by Jews is more than some of them can handle. Often converts become more religious than their born Jewish spouses, which produces tension in their own households and with their Jewish in-laws. These are practical issues for converts and the Jewish community that are just beginning to be recognized.

We will return to a discussion of the community's role in Chapter 5. In the modern U. S. context, the community does have a legitimate concern about the stability of an intermarried relationship.

What does the research indicate about a culturally and religiously mixed couple's chance of building lasting marital bonds?

Stability of the Couple's Relationship

As we previously indicated, the traditional view was that intermarriage produced unstable, divorce-prone relationships. As Sklare observed, "Romantic love is fine, but it can be destroyed by incompatibilities that never before had occasion to rise to the surface or by ethic prejudices that partners were unaware of" (1971, p. 196).

Recent figures put the Jewish-gentile divorce rate at 55 percent, with the Jewish-Jewish rate at 10 percent (Gallob, 1985, p. 20). What kinds of conflicts do intermarrieds face that add stress to their relationship? As indicated in Chapter 1, negative reactions by Jewish in-laws, by Jewish leaders, and by the Jewish community may eventually take their toll (Gallob, March 6, 1986, p. 25; Gallob, September 25, 1986, p. 21). If children are born, further conflicts are likely over the education and identity of the children. Since most couples attempt a blended approach, they may find either the Christian or the Jewish relatives having a greater influence than they anticipated. Areas of potential conflict include the following:

Amount of involvement with Jews and with gentiles
Art
Communication styles
Foods
Health concerns
Holidays
Interest and concern about anti-Semitism
Interest in Israel
Interest in the Holocaust
Jokes
Life cycle events
Music
Parental contact
Political power concerns
Raising of children
Role beliefs

To overcome problems associated with these areas of potential disagreement, couples must work extra hard in their marriage and exercise considerable good will and tolerance. Certainly joint religious practices and community involvements can aid a couple's unity. Interestingly, our data showed more reported disagreements over religion among the in-married than the convert marriages. The five divorced converts who responded did not significantly differ from married converts.

SUMMARY OF COMPARISONS

The data presented in this chapter give us comparative information to put convert behavior into a realistic perspective. It also gives us a picture of the characteristics of the Jewish partner.

We found that the Jewish partners tended to be upper-middle-class professionals. They had very good relationships with their well-educated parents. They were exposed early to interacting with gentiles and had gentile friends in adolescence. They had on the average seven and one-half years of Jewish education, although they attended public school. A third remained religiously active as adults, 56 percent were satisfied with Judaism, two-thirds liked Jewish traditions. Fifty-seven percent of them identified with Reform Judaism. Half of their parents initially opposed their intermarriage, though their friends supported it. They disliked Christian services, and 98 percent of them and their parents favored conversion of their gentile partner. They did not view their potential in-laws as very religious, and 58 percent actively encouraged conversion of their mate.

Compared with in-married Jews, the Jewish partner had parents who were more positive toward gentiles. Both the Jewish partner and his gentile mate felt more positive toward his (Jewish) parents than toward his partner's parents, whom they saw less often as well. Surprisingly, our in-marrieds reported more disagreements at home than the out-marrieds.

In comparing converts, in-marrieds, and Jewish partners on their beliefs we found partners to be similar to in-married born Jews, with both dissimilar to the converts on adherence to Jewish, Christian, and ethnic-related beliefs. Converts were more likely to hold traditional Jewish beliefs than their Jewish partners or in-marrieds. Because traditional beliefs in being chosen, having a covenantal relationship with God, being a light to the nations, and expecting the Messiah are stressed in Christian teachings as the heritage that the Jewish people forsake, they are consequently well known to Christians even today.

At the same time, perhaps not surprisingly, converts held more Christian beliefs. Since, unlike Jews, converts tend to believe that Jesus never broke with Judaism, they don't feel a conflict in holding both Jewish and Christian beliefs. (It should be noted, though, that only 10 percent of converts strongly held Christian beliefs. The remainder adhered to a milder, more qualified version of Christian doctrines.)

Converts and Jews stress different ethnic beliefs. Converts seem more concerned with issues that immediately affect them, such as anti-Semitism, while Jews were more concerned with community survival, especially for Israel.

Students' views of what Jews believe did not change as a result of the introductory course. They correctly assess Jews' low adherence to Christian beliefs and high support for in-marriage. They underestimate our religiously involved Jews' holding of religious and especially of ethnic concerns, although the belief patterns attributed to Jews may be a better approximation of the general Jewish community that includes less involved Jews. They wrongly assess themselves as having stronger religious and ethnic beliefs than born-Jews, at least as represented by our study's born Jews.

Self-assessed knowledge of religious practices is similar for all three groups, but converts tend to believe they are more knowledgeable than their partners believe about themselves. Both converts and partners admit to less knowledge of Jewish community resources than did our in-married Jews.

In actual religious practices, our religiously oriented in-marrieds have the highest level of practice, then the Jewish partners, then the converts. However, in ethnic involvements the order tends to be in-marrieds, converts, and then partners. Apparently these converts do provide their household with vital links to the Jewish community that their partner might otherwise miss.

Of greatest concern to the future of the Jewish community is the fact that the convert and her partner share similarly weak views concerning the Jewish embeddedness of their children. They have less concern about their child or children having a Jewish identification, mostly Jewish friends, or a Jewish marital partner. They are also more tolerant of Christian exposures for their children than are in-marrieds, and they prefer that their children be free to choose their own religion.

Our data is generally similar to data from other studies. The partners in our study had more Jewish education, but that may be because other studies report all intermarriages whereas we are focusing on partners whose gentile spouses convert to Judaism. While our converts tend to have lower levels of practice than our religiously active born Jews, they do as well or better on major practices when compared with general Jewish population studies. This suggests that converts are making a needed contribution to the Jewish community. Their practice patterns are respectable when compared with the general Jewish community norms. It seems likely that while they do bring some Christian contacts into their Jewish household, converts also maintain a better than average religious connection and an average ethnic involvement. For conversionary couples, intermarriage appears to be a step into mainstream Judaism, not out of it.

Since we have now looked at the various kinds of information on converts that our study provides, we will turn our attention to making some recommendations based on those findings that we hope will help both potential and actual converts and the Jewish community. Chapter 5 presents that discussion.

5

Conclusions and Recommendations

WHAT CONCLUSIONS CAN one derive from the data and issues covered in our discussion? Is the issue of absorption versus assimilation an important consideration today? Should the Jewish community encourage conversion and, if so, under what conditions? Are there actions that would strengthen the integration of all converts and their children? What are the special needs of persons who convert on their own without a Jewish partner (15 percent in our convert study, 15 percent in a national 1984 study by Mayer, and 8 percent in our student groups)? What about those two-thirds of intermarrieds whose gentile partner does not convert? We now move from the data to what we view as appropriate conclusions.

CONCLUSIONS

There are no easy answers to these important questions that we have posed. On the surface it would appear that even though religion and family have lost most of their power to control behavior and that intermarriages are on the increase, the individual Jew maintains a high Jewish identity. According to Mayer (1987), even among the two-thirds of nonconversionary intermarrieds, 73 percent of Jewish partners retain their Jewish identity. That was not true in the past; for Jews who married gentiles, intermarriage often served as an opportunity to leave a community that was the object of hostility by the majority population and that imposed severe restrictions on Jewish ambitions in many areas of life. Today, though anti-Semitism is by no means eradicated, Jews by and large are not inhibited by their Jewishness and have attained recognition in most areas of American life. In addition, mainline churches, which in the past took every opportunity to convert Jews to Christianity, have now abandoned an organized "mission to Jews." Aggressive missionary efforts aimed at Jews are limited to a few fundamentalist Christian groups. American Jews are generally accepted, or at least tolerated, by the majority and secure and proud in their own identity. It would thus seem that we could conclude that U.S. Jews should have little concern about being assimilated by others and thus not be alarmed by intermarriage.

Actually, the absorption ability of the Jewish community requires more than personal security and a sense of pride in a Jewish identity. An intense commitment and energetic involvement is required by Jews if that identity is to be transmitted, otherwise Jewish life will be vulnerable to the forces of assimilation. As Kaplan stated, "When the contacts [between groups] result in inter-marriage, and children are born, the more vigorous civilization will be the one to which the children will belong" (1934/1957, p. 97). In fact the vital element of Jewish commitment is not a new consider-ation in the absorption/assimilation formula that we have posited. The strength of the Jewish community to absorb outsiders and its ability to resist attempts by others to overwhelm it have always come from an energetic, dynamic, and committed community. A convert joining such a community would absorb the commitment of the community and of his or her new Jewish in-laws.

What type of community and family is the convert joining today? Do the facts indicate a committed community and family or do they reveal a Jewish community with a minimal and superficial commit-ment?

Those who discourage conversion to Judaism argue that whereas it is true that currently Jewish identity in the United States seems to be secure and that there is a lessening of forces that formerly drove Jews away from the Jewish community, nevertheless that gain is offset by a weakening of commitment that is evident in contem-porary Jewish life. Consequently, the pessimists believe that the expectation that current converts can be absorbed by the Jewish community is not justified. From this view, the fragile identity of the modern Jewish community cannot withstand intermarriages. Who will be the role model for the convert? Pessimists can point to our study to bolster their argument that in a mostly weakly com-mitted Jewish community, converts would only further reflect and increase that weak commitment. To cite just a few discouraging examples from the data: 51 percent of the converts would not be concerned if their children married out of the faith/group; the extent of their knowledge about the Jewish community is minimal; only 17 percent report being regularly engaged in any form of adult Jewish education; and only 22 percent regularly attend synagogue Sabbath services. It would also be of concern that 80 percent of the converts are involved in secular aspects of Christmas, and as many as 10 percent retain some traditional Christian views even after conversion. These examples from our data certainly do not describe a group who would engage in the Jewish community's battle against assimilation but describe a group that would likely hasten its demise.

Others, more optimistically, can counter the above arguments by interpreting the Jewish condition and our data differently. We have ascertained, they would say, that Jews identify proudly with the Jewish community, which even by itself is an important commitment. Converts, they would say, not only reflect the standards of the general community, but at least some bring with them an even greater commitment. It is remarkable, they would argue, that after a rather short period of study, converts identify personally with the Jewish community. Though more than 80 percent began study attached to a Jewish partner, 82 percent considered themselves to be the prime initiators of their decision to convert. In many areas of religious observance they equal or surpass born Jews. They celebrate holidays in great numbers; for example, Hanukah (82 percent), Passover (85 percent), High Holiday services (80 percent), fasting on Yom Kippur (67 percent), Sabbath lighting of candles (47 percent), and recitation of *Kiddush* (34 percent); two-thirds belong to a synagogue, and 63 percent at least sometimes participate in Jewish adult education. Of course there is room for increasing involvement, but this represents a substantial beginning. Furthermore, what alternative is available to the Jewish community? It is either intermarriage without conversion or conversionary intermarriage. Intermarriage is an established fact that is unlikely to diminish in the free society in which we live. In fact the most recent data indicate a rise to more than 70 percent intermarriage for young Jews in major metropolitan centers (Gallob, 1988). The behavior of current converts as a group who receive minimal formal support is at least as good as that of born Jews as a group. Therefore, from a realistic point of view, the community can expect to maintain some stability and to decrease its losses if it encourages conversion and supports converts.

RECOMMENDATIONS

What are our recommendations based on our reading of the data and on our experience with converts and the conversion process? We propose that ways can and should be found to develop imaginative programs that will further strengthen converts' vital integration into the most active and committed segment of the Jewish community and that may help to draw greater numbers of intermarrieds to seek conversion. We make the following suggestions:

1. We call for the unconditional acceptance of the potential and actual convert by the Jewish family and by the Jewish community. Conversion is not to be looked upon as a compromise solution after all attempts have failed to discourage marriage between a Jew and a non-Jew. Our study shows that 46 percent of Jewish fathers and 47 percent of Jewish mothers are seen by the gentile partner as either disapproving of or neutral to the marriage of their child to a person who is willing to convert to Judaism; 18 percent of Jewish fathers and 14 percent of Jewish mothers are perceived as not supporting the conversion. Our data also showed that nonconverting gentile partners reported even more negative reactions. The message undoubtedly colors the family relationship from its very inception and discourages the non-Jew from commencing conversion studies, or, if they are undertaken, the potentially positive effects of the conversion may be reduced. Conversion, as we have indicated, in a short period of time places the convert on a par with the general Jewish community's practice and involvement. In the answers to our question "What do you like *least* about your experience with Jews and Judaism?" it became clear that the struggle to be fully accepted was a significant negative issue for the respondents. Almost a third of them perceived the Jewish community as generally negative toward converts and conversion. The following comments are instructive:

> I don't like people who make their cutting remarks . . . "Oh, you wouldn't understand because you've converted" . . . who feel as if they need to keep you at arms' length.
> I dislike that I will never be Jewish to some because I was not born a Jew.
> Jews always think of me as a non-Jew or not a "real Jew."

How much more efficacious would their conversion be if these converts sense an enthusiastic welcome and support for their continuing education by the Jewish community and the Jewish family. How many are discouraged from converting because of such negative views? Jews need to understand that in the Christian community from which these people come, potential converts are lovingly wooed and supported, and those who convert are fully accepted, highly valued, and aided in numerous ways. Jews need help from the leadership level on down to confront their negative stereotypes and to develop more positive understandings about and approaches to drawing in intermarrieds in general and converts in particular. We call upon the community to develop sensitivity sessions between converts and born Jews, workshops, lectures, and other programs aimed at helping Jews become more positive toward these strangers in their midst. As Mayer points out, Jews are not very good in socializing outsiders:

> All minorities have difficulty being accepted as full-fledged equals in their host cultures, as we Jews, of all people, should know. This problem is all the more true for Jews by choice who must be integrated into Jewish culture and society which has not had the experience of integrating outsiders for nearly two thousand years (1983, p. 68).

2. While our data indicate that the Introduction to Judaism course is looked upon favorably by the converts, there is room for improvement. Many communities lack such organized efforts and should seek to establish them, using the Chicago course as a model. (However, our data indicate that the Chicago course itself could benefit from several changes, which we will discuss.) Besides participation by the potential convert, the Chicago course requires the Jewish partner to attend the class. The results have been gratifying and of significant help to the potential convert. By attending the same classes, partners are stimulated to discuss the issues and ideas raised and to develop a joint understanding. Through the course, Jewish partners often find new connections to Judaism that strengthen their own Jewish identity, commitment, and observance. One convert replying to our study appended a note saying, "My husband, who had attended Hebrew school, learned a tremendous amount in the class. He is more religious [now] due to our experience together in my conversion." Why not extend the class participation to include the parental Jewish family that the convert will join?

We also suggest that experiential sessions become an integral part of the course, such as a weekend retreat that could enable the group to exchange ideas and experiences on an informal basis, observe the Sabbath together, and interact in a joyous and meaningful setting. A group Sabbath experience could also encourage Sabbath and holiday attendance in students' synagogues. The class might also arrange group "field trips" to local synagogues to help students experience a variety of Jewish services within the various branches of Judaism. Such group worship experiences could be enhanced by prior discussion of the format and rituals they will see and by a postdiscussion of their observations, reactions, and questions. Group cultural trips could be an important addition as well.

From our data, introductory courses need to provide more discussion of the ethnic dimensions and issues for potential converts. Christians understand religious conversion but not ethnic integration, and thus they need guidelines to consider as they make changes in their lives. They need to have a better understanding of the tie between family rituals and the family closeness and unity of Jews that they are drawn to. Such understanding should help them incorporate and adapt Jewish home rituals, especially for Sabbath, into their family life. Sociological research on strong families clearly documents the value of home-centered rituals in developing family strength and unity. Frequent, regular family rituals are not just religiously important, they help stabilize families in an atomistic world such as ours.

More discussion of community concerns and reactions about intermarriage and conversion needs to be held so potential converts can understand the full context for the reactions they encounter, and so they can decide for themselves how best to address those concerns in their own lives. In particular, in a culture that stresses individual rights, discussion of issues concerning the needs and rights of the Jewish community should be explicitly addressed, especially as they relate to Christian beliefs, Christmas involvements, child Jewish socialization, and child friend/dating/marriage issues.

3. Committed members of the Jewish community, and preferably the immediate Jewish family if qualified in their commitment, should be recruited to serve as role models/mentors for intermarried and conversionary families. Currently without a systematic way of ensuring that non-Jews and converts are exposed to the best of Jewish traditions, their experiences are often counterproductive. For example, it is discouraging to teach the Introduction to Judaism course directed to potential converts on the week following the

Passover seder. Prior to the holiday they have studied the Passover *Haggadah* with its rituals and anticipated the forthcoming seder with all its rich symbolism, discussions of freedom, and warm fellowship; their expectation is to be uplifted spiritually. The impression gained from the seder is often quite the opposite of their anticipation. The leader conducting the seder is described as one "racing through the *Haggadah*." The family and guests, instead of discussing the meaning of freedom, are impatient for the meal, and the entire evening lacks spirituality. In truth, the actual seder has no resemblance to the seder they learned about in their studies. Their experience can be summarized by a parody in the play *Beau Jeste*, where the total ceremony is limited to the statement, "We were slaves, and we were freed; now let's eat." The community should seek authentic role models who would adopt a convert for at least a year. These knowledgeable families should invite converts and their spouses for Sabbath dinners, holiday celebrations, synagogue and community offerings, lectures, and social events.

Such an organized support effort could aid converts in becoming integrated into the life of the Jewish community and into the best of its home-oriented rituals. A people who want to perpetuate their future and thus assure their creative survival need to invest time and effort with new Jews and not force them to fend for themselves. The Jewish community has already developed imaginative programs for the integration of Soviet Jewry that are bearing fruit. Those programs could serve as models for similar support offered to potential and actual converts. It cannot be assumed that their Jewish partner or in-laws, if they have them, will be able to provide the intensive mentoring they need to firmly establish themselves as Jews. At the very most, intermarrieds have only one Jewish family to call on instead of two. For those without attachment to a Jewish partner, the need for a mentoring Jewish family is even stronger. And even nonconversionary intermarrieds could likely use some role models, perhaps other intermarrieds who have evidenced strong Jewish commitments. A systematic, well-organized program is required to truly absorb converts into the Jewish community. And to make the route less difficult and more supportive and attractive may well draw others of the two-thirds who presently do not convert.

4. Ongoing support programs should be made available for converts and their spouses. Paul and Rachael Cowen, the authors of *Mixed Blessings* (1987), have increased our awareness of the possible frictions that emerge periodically in a conversionary marriage,

particularly prior to Christmas-Hanukah and Easter-Passover, which evoke childhood memories and nostalgia. Our data also confirm that former beliefs do not necessarily disappear with conversion, so that one out of ten converts maintain major Christian beliefs, and the vast majority celebrate Christmas as a secular holiday. Some who answered our Study of Judaism Survey were frank in their responses. One wrote, "It is very difficult to completely abandon a religion you have grown up with." Another wrote, "Becoming a Jew and practicing as a Jew have been very overwhelming. . . . Judaism for me will only be my religion, and while [religion] is important, my identity as a Southerner will always be paramount." It is difficult for converts to erase their past. This can lead to creative infusions, as one convert remarked, "I enjoy taking the best aspects of my past traditions and incorporating them into a Jewish context. For example, when my daughter was named at Temple, she wore a beautiful gown, sort of like Christening. . . ." Or the difficulty in knowing what to adapt and what to delete can lead to less benign syncretizations, such as a "Hanukah bush" or to other problems for the conversionary household. We urge that the community provide a place for converts to ventilate their feelings and resolve the tensions inherent in a conversion process.

Former converts and their spouses could be recruited to act as "Big Buddies" to fledgling intermarrieds. Formal support networks should be organized among course participants rather than left to chance. Students should be told about the outreach and follow-up programs sponsored by Reform Judaism, and those programs should be expanded to Conservative converts.

A trained rabbi and a therapist should be available for individual and group counseling of converts and their families as needed. The time spent in discussing the dilemmas intermarrieds will face is, of necessity, very limited in any introductory course. Problems, doubts, and tensions often occur and reoccur after conversion. Rabbis and mental health workers can jointly formulate a program of counseling. The divorce rate is much higher for intermarriages (55 percent) than for in-marriages (10 percent). The community in such divorces stands to lose not only the convert but also the children. And "spiritual custody" battles do no one good. A nonthreatening, readily available counseling program could help intermarrieds understand that difficulties are the norm, are to be expected, and can be supportively handled.

A convert-oriented monthly or quarterly newsletter could be initiated at the local level to inform converts of relevant community programs and services and to discuss Jewish seasonal, ethnic, and other issues, to frankly face common problems experienced by converts, and to aid converts' knowledge, identity, and integration.

5. Synagogues have special obligations to aid in the integration of the convert. The initial contact of potential converts through the final ceremony of conversion is entrusted to the hands of the rabbinate. It is encouraging that our data show that 69 percent of converts are affiliated with the synagogue. This is a slightly higher percentage than the 60 percent for born Jews. Synagogues should undertake special efforts to increase the converts' appreciation of and involvement in Judaism. The synagogue should encourage converts to make up the life cycle events that they have missed. Some life cycle events are required of converts as part of the conversion process; for example, basic studies in Judaism, circumcision or *hatafat dam brit,* immersion, and taking a Hebrew name. However, we suggest that other life cycle events should also be encouraged for converts, such as a public naming and conversion recognition ceremony, the public naming and dedication of any children in the relationship, a reaffirmation in a Jewish marriage ceremony for one that took place prior to conversion, and the *bar* or *bat mitzvah.* These events could become community celebrations. Not only could participation make up for Jewish life cycle events that were missed, but it would also provide additional years of study and serve as a message that the synagogue values its converts and wants to help them be involved in greater participation in the religious, cultural, and social life of the synagogue and to deepen their religious commitment. The synagogue should provide classes for converts to learn Hebrew, the prayers, the daily service, holiday services, and home rituals. Besides religiously oriented instruction, classes for learning common Jewish songs, dances, stories, games, and even jokes that are taught to children could be initiated for converts. Cooking classes focusing on recipes for the major holidays are another resource that converts could utilize.

Such classes could be of use to born Jews as well as to converts, thus making them viable for synagogues with small numbers of converts. In communities where individual synagogues cannot afford to provide these supports, classes could be jointly or centrally run instead.

6. We suggest that the continuing education of the convert be-

come the responsibility of the organized Jewish community. The conversion ceremony should be viewed not as the culmination of the Jewish experience but as its beginning. It is true that Hillel, a rabbi often quoted in the Talmud, participated in the conversion of a proselyte who wished to know all about Judaism while standing on one foot, but even Hillel, who summarized the essence of Judaism in his famous statement, "What is distasteful to you do not do to others," added, "The rest is commentary, now go and study." In the Jewish tradition, the very rituals of conversion, such as circumcision and immersion in water, signify that converts become newly born. The message of the tradition is that a proselyte is a neophyte in the understanding of Judaism and, like any child, is called upon to increase his or her knowledge.

An organized program of ongoing Jewish studies and reading should be made readily available. A variety of learning formats should be developed on topics such as the prayers, the services, the Passover rituals, traditional religious and ethnic music, Jewish history, Jewish humor, and current issues. Some examples of learning aids are instructional tapes, video programs such as "Civilization and the Jews" and "When Love Meets Tradition" (developed by the Reform branch), mail-in study programs, or at least bibliographies and resource information sheets on relevant topics. Some of this material is already available, but converts need to become aware of it and provided easy access, and some new material needs developing. Perhaps synagogue or Jewish community center libraries could be expanded to include such resources for loan.

A year's tuition scholarship to Spertus College of Judaica or its equivalent could be paid by the Jewish community. Besides a tuition scholarship for some, a Jewish magazine gift subscription could be given to all participants in the introductory course. A local Jewish publication such as *The Sentinel* and/or a national Jewish magazine such as *Moment* could be most helpful in aiding the converts' understanding and knowledge about Jewish life. They would sense by reading the periodical both the dynamism of Jewish life and its resources—its debates, its news, its cultural activities, its bookstores, its restaurants, and so on.

There needs to be some effort at investigating why such a large number of converts acknowledge the importance of and their interest in continuing their Jewish education, but so few (17 percent) regularly do so. Efforts can then be more clearly directed at overcoming those obstacles. Such supportive measures would go a long way to help converts learn about the Jewish community and to partake of its resources and issues. Even considered on practical grounds, a modest investment could reap large dividends for the community in encouraging the involvement of converts in its life. A recent "Book of Life," a publication of the Chicago Jewish Federation indicating the annual monetary gifts to the Jewish United Fund, contains the names of Soviet Jews who made significant contributions only a few years after settling in Chicago. These people were helped by the Federation to immigrate and settle in the area. To show their appreciation, the new Jewish Americans have become contributors to the Federation's fund-raising campaigns.

7. For a limited time after their conversion (say three to five years) it would be wise to consider converts a distinct group entitled to preferential and supportive treatment. We are well aware of the admonition in the Jewish tradition that one is prohibited from reminding a convert of her or his former status and that one must not differentiate between a born Jew and a proselyte. This policy was established to prevent negative discrimination and second-class citizenship for converts. Rather, we propose positive, special treatment as a kind of "internship" in Judaism. To encourage the ethnic identification of converts, we suggest special "convert missions to Israel" to enable them to spend meaningful time in a totally Jewish setting and thereby deepen their Jewish identity. Jews themselves have had enough experience to know the value to the community, both spiritually and financially, of people touched by Israel through their participation in missions. If convert-only missions cannot be offered, then converts could be given subsidies in order to participate in trips to Israel organized by other groups from the community.

Those applying for the subsidies could be required to pursue a study program prior to their departure for Israel. We envision six months of weekly preparatory classes to qualify for the mission. Lectures on the history of ancient Israel, Zionism, and modern Israel and a taste of the *ulpan* method for studying the Hebrew language would enhance converts' appreciation of Israel. Such classes could be open even to those unable to actually travel to Israel and to born Jews as well. Non-traveling participants could receive reports and see pictures from the travelers' experiences to stimulate them vicariously. We are aware that not everyone would participate in such programs, but those who did would be immensely enriched, and, in the long run, the Jewish community would be the beneficiary.

Locally, special federation mini-missions could be run to introduce potential and new converts to community resources and programs. The Chicago Federation has organized successful mini-missions for rabbis, elected board members of the Federation, contributors, and others. Why not a "mini-mission" for new Jews? The community can point to its many activities with pride; why keep them a secret from Jews by choice? The support given to the Jewish centers, educational networks, programs for the aged, aid to the poor, and family counseling services could be made part of the awareness of new Jews by direct experience. Jewish networks would be expanded for those joining the community.

It must be kept in mind that these young professional families tend not to live in highly Jewish areas. Consequently, programs to help them develop ethnic awareness, identifications, and networks need to be planned, perhaps as part of ongoing "refresher" or follow-up postcourse group events. In addition, those converts without partners (10 percent to 20 percent) need help to enter the Jewish singles scene and the aid of "matchmakers," since most people meet their spouse through friend and family introductions.

8. Children of out-marriages require special attention. Our study, though limited because of the age of the children, points to potentially disturbing facts. It is understandable that converts would find it difficult to send a message to their children that they would oppose intermarriage or that they would stand in the way of a child's choice of religion. We found that 79 percent of converts would encourage their children to make their own choice of religion, 83 percent are certain they would not restrict their children's dating to Jews (another 14 percent are unsure; only 3 percent indicate they actually plan on restrictions), and 72 percent believe that restrictions are not important. If the message that they should embrace Judaism and marry a Jew can't come decisively from the parents, should it not come from the Jewish community?

The Jewish community must find ways to deepen the Jewish identity and commitment of children of conversionary marriages. We suggest that scholarships be made available to children of converts for attendance at Jewish day schools, Jewish camps, and a junior year in Israel. The community should do no less for the children of converts than it already does for children of Russian immigrants who currently are granted scholarships to day schools and camps. The convert and the conversionary family are also recent "arrivals" to the Jewish community.

The introductory course should be organized to spend explicit time on issues concerning how to raise a Jewish child. Our data show that this concern is not addressed and that converts do not increase their commitments to Jewish child-rearing over the course of study or in comparison with nonconverts. Discussion should be planned about issues of Jewish survival and transmission of identity, the importance and handling of friend and dating relationships, and the conflicts between tolerance of other groups and of in-marriage requirements. Because of the complexities of the issues, ongoing seminars, workshops, and discussion groups on child-rearing issues for various ages of children need to be offered by the community. Born Jews are just as likely to benefit from these kinds of parental supports and should be invited as well to share their struggles and successes.

Volunteer Jewish grandfathers and grandmothers might provide helpful, secondary inputs, models, and supports to conversionary children in their impressionable seven- to sixteen-year-old years. Like born Jews, conversionary family children would then have two sets of Jewish grandparents from whom to learn stories, traditions, and attitudes.

9. Converts can be asked to serve as a bridge to the non-Jewish community. Obviously because of their circle of non-Jewish friends and family they are in a position to become ambassadors of good will in the general community and thus help break down the stereotypes about Jews that are still prevalent. Rabbis have found converts to be effective in many such areas. Quite recently, in an experience with a school system, a particularly recalcitrant teacher failed to recognize the distress of Jewish parents when he demanded that a major examination be given on Yom Kippur. An indignant convert, without the baggage of self-consciousness that many Jews carry, demanded the postponement of tests on religious grounds. What the Jewish community couldn't do, she accomplished in one session with the principal, and the matter was settled in an amicable fashion. We suggest that in areas of public relations, interdenominational activities, and Israel concerns, converts' active presence and leadership should be sought.

Converts can also be asked to lead discussions on Christianity and Christian perspectives to inform the Jewish community. Jews themselves often hold false views of Christian doctrines, concerns, and issues and are unaware of the diversity within Christianity or of changes in Christian attitudes and teachings about Jews. Converts could be helpful in working with junior high and high school Jewish children to help them understand the important differences between Christians and Jews, to discuss how to answer Christian missionaries, and to share the value of choosing to be a Jew.

10. Finally, we suggest that the Shavuot holiday commemorating the Sinaitic revelation and the proclamation of the Ten Commandments be established as a day for honoring the thousands of Jews by choice who have joined the Jewish fold. The Jewish community should not overlook the element of heroism and risk it takes for one to convert to Judaism in the twentieth century. A person living in the century of the Holocaust surely is aware that to become a Jew is to join a community that is vulnerable to discrimination and persecution and thus deserves recognition for that courageous act.

The festival of Shavuot, with its emphasis on Jews' receiving the Torah for the first time and the traditional reading of the book of Ruth, the classic convert to Judaism, would be the logical and appropriate place for such tributes to Jews by choice. A new ritual could be developed such as calling only Jews by choice to the Torah, having converts read from the book of Ruth, having the service including the sermon be handled by conversionary intermarrieds, and having converts relate their Jewish experiences. Such a ceremony could enhance converts' acceptance and lift the morale of the congregants.

Having made these recommendations, it should be apparent that we, as the authors of the study, believe that a deeper commitment on the part of the Jewish community to its own religious spirituality and its institutions would reflect itself in a greater commitment by Jews by choice. Should we aggressively seek to convert gentiles to Judaism? Our opinion is that we should continue to revere the saying of Hillel, "What is distasteful to you do not do to others." Jews have always been uncomfortable with those who wished to convert them to other faiths. That discomfort turned to anger when missionaries proclaimed that "there is no salvation outside the church." No such doctrine exists in Judaism. On the contrary, less is required to attain salvation for a gentile than it is for a Jew. According to rabbinic tradition, a Jew is obligated to observe 613 commandments; a non-Jew is required to observe only seven Noachide Laws (*Sanhedrin* 56–60; Genesis, Chapter 9). These laws are mainly in the moral sphere—avoiding bloodshed, sexual sins, theft, cruelty to animals, idolatry, and blasphemy, and establishing a legal system. Maimonides taught that one who observes these laws has a share in the world to come even without becoming a Jew and is entitled to the highest earthly honors (*Encyclopedia Judaica*, 1956, p. 358). However, if a gentile wishes to become a Jew, the doors should always be open without reservations and the community should warmly accept Jews by choice. As in the time of the Second Commonwealth, gentiles should be attracted to Judaism because of the enthusiastic involvement and excitement about Jewish life exhibited by Jews themselves. Certainly the option of conversion should be discussed with the gentile by the Jewish partner and by the potential in-laws, but the discussion should be without coercion. If an intermarriage does occur without conversion, as much support as possible for a Jewish life-style should be afforded those couples who comprise two-thirds of the intermarrieds. And the door should remain open for conversion at a later time. Mayer's data (1987) and ours both indicate that of the one-third of intermarrieds who currently convert, one-fourth do so only after the birth of their first child, and another fourth even later, usually before the child's *bar* or *bat mitzvah*.

Thus far, our recommendations have been directed to the Jewish community. We are aware that the suggestions we've made can be implemented on a piece-meal and partial basis or, worse, not at all, by each Jewish community. However, we believe the current situation warrants central planning and coordination. The Reform movement has already established a commission on outreach directed by Lydia Kukoff, herself a convert. That commission, along with local outreach efforts, has already begun to develop some materials and programs along the lines we have suggested. We call on all segments of Judaism to cooperate in developing the work done by Reform outreach. They certainly have seen a payoff from the limited efforts they have made thus far, since the majority of converts are to Reform Judaism. We hope our work will give impetus to a stronger cooperative effort using the model of Reform outreach and of Federation-sponsored programs for Soviet Jews. Much of what we've recommended would benefit born Jews, if they were invited to participate (as they should be), as well as intermarrieds and converts. Recently Tobin, who has researched and written about intermarriage for some time, made a number of suggestions for strengthening the commitment and viability of born Jews as a method of influencing the rates of out-marriage without conversion. He concluded, "A vital

Judaism can thrive in the openness of American society if we light Shabbat candles, not Yahrzeit candles in the face of intermarriage" (1990, p. 63). The programs we suggest are in keeping with his recommendations for actions to increase the value of Judaism and the Jewish experience for born Jews.

Finally, we want to address a few remarks to potential and actual converts to Judaism. The process of becoming a Jew is a process of resocialization, not just learning a few new religious holiday rituals. Converts indicate that even in the religious realm, major changes in life-style and beliefs are required. In addition, the ethnic dimension, "feeling, talking, reacting like a Jew," and being accepted as a Jew by Jews, takes even more time and effort. A commitment to lifelong study and involvement must be made and followed through. The potential convert would also be wise to heed the advice of one who went through the process and who made the following statement in the questionnaire returned to us:

> Make sure that you are converting for yourself and not a mate or a future mate. It is very hard to be a Jew, and you need a real commitment to be a Jew by choice. . . . Remember you have gone down a very difficult road to get where you are . . . search your soul.

It is our opinion that to become Jewish in order to have a unified household is a legitimate first step, but as Hillel said to the gentile, *"V'iduch zil gmor,"* ("The rest go and study"). That rest of Judaism must be acquired through intensified emotional and rational study. And raising Jewishly committed children who will marry a Jew or convert to Judaism is the ultimate proof of the seriousness and effectiveness of that commitment. Only then can the convert, a Jew by choice, truly say, "Your people are my people, and your God is my God," and the Jewish community will answer, "Amen."

Appendix: Supplemental Tables for Chapter 4

TABLE 4.3
COMPARISONS AMONG BORN JEWS' (BJ), PARTNERS' (PR), AND CONVERTS' (CV) BACKGROUND PUSH FACTORS

Push Variables	Means			Significant Differences*		
	Born Jews	Partners	Converts	BJ vs. PR	BJ vs. CV	PR vs. CV
Sex	0.54	0.27	0.80			+
Age	47.45	33.35	35.17	–	–	–
Adolescent Relationship to Father	3.27	3.10	2.68		–	–
Adolescent Relationship to Mother	3.34	3.40	2.95		–	–
Father's View of Jews	4.42	4.26	2.44		–	–
Mother's View of Jews	4.32	4.32	2.55		–	–
Father's View of Gentiles	2.60	2.76	NA	+		
Mother's View of Gentiles	2.27	2.76	NA	+		
Father's Gentile Friends	2.41	2.67	NA	+		
Mother's Gentile Friends	2.18	2.67	NA	+		

Father's Religious Activity	2.33	2.26	1.95		+	+
Mother's Religious Activity	1.93	2.19	2.61		+	+
Childhood Religious Involvement	2.50	2.64	3.14		+	+
Years of Formal Religious Instruction	2.48	7.62	7.05	+	+	−
Years of Formal Religious School	1.10	1.06	2.86		+	+
Dissatisfaction with Childhood Religion	2.56	2.56	1.29		−	+
Adult View about Jesus as Divine	0.76	0.93	1.29		+	+
Total, Questioning about God**	10.48	10.13	11.44	−	+	+
Total, Childhood Major Rabbinic Religious Practices**	6.35	7.23	NA	+		
Total, Childhood Supportive Rabbinic Religious Practices**	5.50	6.14	NA	+		
Total, Childhood Christian Practices**	1.42	1.97	NA	+		
Total, Childhood Knowledge of Primary Blessings**	2.92	3.41	NA	+		
Total, Childhood Ethnic Inputs**	1.93	2.35	NA	+		

* "−" indicates that the comparision score is significantly lower than the born Jews' score; in the case of PR vs. CV, partners represent born Jews.

"+" indicates that the comparison score is significantly higher than the born Jews' score; in the case of PR vs. CV, partners represent born Jews.

** A description of the Total (scale) variables can be obtained from Dr. Forster.

TABLE 4.4

COMPARISONS AMONG BORN JEWS' (BJ), PARTNERS' (PR), AND CONVERTS' (CV) BACKGROUND PULL FACTORS

	Means			Significant Differences*		
Pull Variables	Born Jews	Partners	Converts	BJ vs. PR	BJ vs. CV	PR vs. CV
Partner's Family Relationship Compared with Own Family	NA	0.80	1.49			+
Get Along with Partner's Father	3.34	1.06	1.08	–	–	
Get Along with Partner's Mother	2.75	0.91	0.97	–	–	
See Partner's Family	3.44	2.99	3.46	–		+
See Own Family	3.78	3.61	3.39		–	–
Disagree with Partner	2.41	2.01	2.06	–	–	
Considered Converting to Christianity	0.11	0.09	NA			
Belief That Conversion Is Important to Be Part of the Jewish Community	NA	3.42	3.84			+

Converts Accepted by Jews	3.62	3.41	2.93		—	—
Converts Are Serious About Being a Jew	2.51	2.56	NA			
Converts Are Observant	2.24	2.25	NA			
Converts Are Observant as Jews	2.24	2.74	2.60	+	+	+
Converts Are Involved in the Jewish Community	2.13	2.05	NA			
Converts Are as Active as Jews	2.29	2.50	2.07		—	—
Difficulty in Being a Convert	0.89	0.82	1.99	+	+	+
Difficulty in Being a Jew	1.53	1.53	NA			—
Converts Contribute to Judaism	3.22	3.49	3.28	+		
Like Converts	4.38	4.70	NA	+		
Jews Understand Converts	2.72	2.17	2.58	—		
Rabbi Supports Converts	4.83	4.74	4.81			
A Jewish Identity Is Personally Important	3.73	3.62	3.04		—	—

* "—" indicates that the comparison score is significantly lower than the born Jews' score; in the case of PR vs CV, partners represent born Jews.

"+" indicates that the comparison score is significantly higher than the born Jews' score; in the case of PR vs. CV, partners represent born Jews.

TABLE 4.5
COMPARISONS AMONG BORN JEWS' (BJ), PARTNERS' (PR), AND CONVERTS' (CV) BELIEF PATTERNS

Belief Variables**	Means			Significant Differences*		
	Born Jews	Partners	Converts	BJ vs. PR	BJ vs. CV	PR vs. CV
General Religious Beliefs						
Often Talk About Religion	2.44(1)	1.64(6)	1.93(5)	−	−	
Frequently Feel Close to God	2.23(2)	2.57(1)	2.62(1)		+	
Prayer Is Important	1.90(3)	1.80(4)	2.39(4)		+	+
Believe in God as Father	1.87(4)	2.22(3)	2.50(2)	+	+	
Religion Influences Daily Life	1.82(5)	1.72(5)	1.57(6)			−
Experience Presence of Divine in Life	1.70(6)	2.54(2)	2.40(3)	+	+	
Jewish Religious Beliefs						
Humans Have Free Will to Choose Good	3.43(1)	2.69(6)	3.44(1)	−		+
Judaism Has More Truth Than Other Religions	3.32(2)	2.94(4)	3.15(3)	−		
There Is Only One God	2.75(3)	3.03(3)	3.24(2)	+	+	+
Beliefs Don't Matter, A Moral Life Does	2.64(4)	2.25(9)	2.44(9)	+		
Jesus' Messiahship Was a Creation of the Early Church	2.59(5)	4.34(1)	2.46(8)	+		−
God Promised the Land of Israel to the Jews	2.47(6)	3.30(2)	2.67(6)	+		
Jews Have a Covenantal Relationship with God	2.46(7)	2.66(7)	2.89(4)		+	
Rabbinic Interpretations Are Valid	2.04(8)	2.38(8)	2.64(5)		+	
Jews Are Chosen to Be a Light to the Nations	1.99(9)	2.04(10)	2.19(10)			
The Hebrew Bible is God's Revealed Word	1.78(10)	2.70(5)	2.51(7)		+	+
Moral Non-Jews Will Be Saved	1.71(11)	1.87(11)	2.16(11)		+	
God Will Send the Messiah at Time's End	1.61(12)	1.83(12)	1.94(12)		+	+
Total, Acceptance of Major Rabbinical Beliefs*	29.09	29.57	31.02			

	In-married Born Jews					
Christian Religious Beliefs						
Jesus Broke with Judaism	2.44(1)	3.97(1)	2.40(1)	+		−
Jesus Will Return as Messiah	0.57(2)	0.58(4)	1.10(3)		+	+
God Exists as a Trinity	0.49(3)	0.39(6)	1.05(5)		+	+
Jesus Rose from the Dead	0.42(4)	0.40(5)	1.07(4)		+	+
God Revealed Himself in Jesus	0.40(5)	0.90(2)	1.17(2)		+	
The Resurrection Proves Jesus Was the Messiah	0.36(6)	0.79(3)	0.78(6)		+	
Total, Acceptance of Major Christian Beliefs*	2.15	2.17	4.06		+	+
Jewish Ethnic Beliefs						
Feel a Bond to Israel	3.85(1)	3.15(3)	2.48(11)		−	
There Must Always Be a Jewish People	3.80(2)	2.90(7)	3.55(1)		−	+
The U.S. Should Aid Israel	3.64(3)	2.81(8)	2.98(7)	−	−	
Being Jewish Is Personally Important	3.61(4)	3.60(1)	3.22(3)		−	
Want to Be Part of the Jewish Community	3.57(5)	3.26(2)	3.04(5)		−	
Anti-Semitism Is a Problem in the U.S.	3.54(6)	2.72(11)	3.28(2)		−	+
It Is Important to Vote for Politicians Who Support Israel	3.44(7)	3.09(5)	2.74(9)		−	
Feel Comfortable in Jewish Settings	3.37(8)	2.52(12)	3.02(6)	−		
Feel Obliged to Help World Jewry	3.36(9)	3.08(6)	2.94(8)		−	
Have Satisfying Life Goals	3.11(10)	2.80(9)	3.14(4)	−		+
Jewish Parents Should Make Sure Their Kids Don't Marry Non-Jews	2.97(11)	1.55(13)	1.42(13)		−	
The Press is Too Negative about Israel	2.66(12)	2.74(10)	2.18(13)		−	−
The Synagogue Should Help Minorities	1.87(13)	3.10(4)	2.51(10)		+	−
Total, Major Ethnic Involvement Beliefs**	24.26	21.87	20.11		−	−

* "−" indicates that the comparison score is significantly lower than the born Jews' score; in the case of PR vs. CV, partners represent born Jews.

"+" indicates that the comparison score is significantly higher than the born Jews' score; in the case of PR vs. CV, partners represent born Jews.

** Variables are listed within each category from highest to lowest according to the in-married, born Jew mean; bracketed number (for example, (1)) is the rank.

* A description of the Total (scale) variables can be obtained from Dr. Forster.

TABLE 4.6
COMPARISONS AMONG STUDENT PERCEPTIONS OF JEWISH BELIEFS (PJ), STUDENTS' OWN BELIEFS (ST), AND ACTUAL BELIEFS OF PARTNERS (PR) AND BORN JEWS (BJ)

Belief Variables**	Student Perception of Jewish Beliefs*	Actual Beliefs			Significant Differences*		
		Born Jews	Partners	Students	PJ vs. BJ	PJ vs. PR	PJ vs. ST
General Religious Beliefs							
Frequently Feel Close to God	2.19(1)	2.23(2)	2.57(1)	2.74(1)		+	+
Prayer Is Important	2.11(2)	1.90(3)	1.80(4)	2.07(3)		−	
Believe in God as Father	2.07(3)	1.87(4)	2.22(3)	2.11(4)		+	
Often Talk about Religion	1.90(4)	2.44(1)	1.64(6)	1.64(5)	+	−	−
Experience Presence of Divine in Life	1.77(5)	1.70(6)	2.54(2)	2.52(2)	+	+	+
Religion Influences Daily Life	1.00(6)	1.82(5)	1.72(5)	1.61(6)	+	+	+
Jewish Religious Beliefs							
Judaism Has More Truth than Other Religions	2.77(1)	3.32(2)	2.94(4)	3.22(6)	+	+	+
There Is Only One God	2.67(2)	2.75(3)	3.03(3)	3.20(7)		+	+
Jews Have a Covenantal Relationship with God	2.63(3)	2.46(7)	2.66(7)	3.07(8)	−		+
God Promised the Land of Israel to the Jews	2.63(4)	2.47(6)	3.30(2)	3.55(3)	−	+	+
Humans Have Free Will to Choose God	2.45(5)	3.43(1)	2.69(6)	2.67(10)	+	+	+
Rabbinic Interpretations Are Valid	2.36(6)	2.04(8)	2.38(8)	2.64(11)	−		+
The Hebrew Bible Is God's Revealed Word	2.28(7)	1.78(10)	2.70(5)	2.94(9)	−	+	+
Jews Are Chosen to Be a Light to the Nations	2.08(8)	1.99(2)	2.04(10)	3.39(5)			+
Jesus' Messiahship was a Creation of the Early Church	2.03(9)	2.59(5)	4.34(1)	3.52(4)	+	+	+
God Will Send the Messiah at Time's End	1.97(10)	1.61(12)	1.83(12)	4.34(1)	−	+	+

Beliefs Don't Matter, a Moral Life Does	1.79(11)	2.64(4)	2.25(9)	2.05(12)	+	+	+
Moral Non-Jews Will Be Saved	1.60(12)	1.71(11)	1.87(11)	3.93(2)	+	+	+
Christian Religious Beliefs							
Jesus Broke with Judaism	1.76(1)	2.44(1)	3.97(1)	3.37(1)	+	+	+
Jesus Will Return as Messiah	0.43(2)	0.57(2)	0.58(4)	2.30(4)	+	+	+
God Exists as a Trinity	0.39(3)	0.49(3)	0.39(6)	1.72(6)	+		+
God Revealed Himself in Jesus	0.27(4)	0.40(5)	0.90(2)	2.70(3)		+	+
Jesus Rose from the Dead	0.13(5)	0.42(4)	0.40(5)	2.14(5)	+	+	+
The Resurrection Proves Jesus Was the Messiah	0.10(6)	0.36(6)	0.79(3)	3.37(2)	+	+	+
Jewish Ethnic Beliefs							
Being Jewish Is Personally Important	2.80(1)	3.61(4)	3.60(1)	2.91(5)	+	+	+
There Must Always Be Jewish People	2.80(2)	3.80(2)	2.90(7)	2.82(7)	+	+	
Want to Be Part of the Jewish Community	2.67(3)	3.57(5)	3.26(2)	2.69(8)	+	+	
Anti-Semitism Is a Problem in the U.S.	2.66(4)	3.54(6)	2.72(11)	2.59(9)	+		
The U.S. Should Aid Israel	2.63(5)	3.64(3)	2.81(8)	3.06(2)	+	+	+
Feel Obliged to Help World Jewry	2.58(6)	3.36(9)	3.08(6)	2.90(6)	+	+	+
Feel Comfortable in Jewish Settings	2.56(7)	3.37(8)	2.52(12)	2.57(10)	+		
It Is Important to Vote for Politicians Who Support Israel	2.55(8)	3.44(7)	3.09(5)	3.12(1)	+	+	+
Have Satisfying Life Goals	2.32(9)	3.11(10)	2.80(9)	2.61(11)	+	+	+
The Press Is Too Negative about Israel	2.08(10)	2.66(12)	2.74(10)	3.01(3)	+	+	+
Jewish Parents Should Make Sure Their Kids Don't Marry Non-Jews	2.05(11)	2.97(11)	1.55(13)	1.29(13)	+		−
The Synagogue Should Help Minorities	1.86(12)	1.87(13)	3.10(4)	3.00(4)	+	+	+
Feel a Bond to Israel	0.65(13)	3.85(1)	3.15(3)	1.78(12)	+	+	+

* "−" indicates that the comparison actual belief score is significantly lower than the perceived Jewish belief score.

"+" indicates that the comparison actual belief score is significantly higher than the perceived Jewish belief score.

** Variables are listed within each category from highest to lowest according to the perceived Jewish belief scores; bracketed number (for example, (1)) is the rank.

\# Post-course and post-only course data used for students' perceived and own beliefs.

TABLE 4.7
COMPARISONS AMONG BORN JEWS' (BJ), PARTNERS' (PR), AND CONVERTS' (CV) KNOWLEDGE

Knowledge Variables**	Means			Significant Differences*		
	Born Jews	Partners	Converts	BJ vs. PR	BJ vs. CV	PR vs. CV
Jewish Religious Beliefs						
Jewish View of God	2.42(1)	2.56(1)	2.80(1)		+	+
Controversy on Who is a Jew	2.37(2)	2.40(2)	2.58(2)		+	
Conservative Judaism	2.17(3)	1.99(6)	2.16(6)	−		+
Orthodox Judaism	2.03(4)	1.89(7)	1.95(8)	−		
View of Jesus	2.01(5)	2.09(4)	2.47(3)		+	+
View of Christianity	1.98(6)	2.06(5)	2.35(4)		+	
Reform Judaism	1.96(7)	2.10(3)	2.35(5)		+	
The Talmud	1.47(8)	1.63(8)	2.00(7)		+	+
Jewish Practice Requirements						
Passover Seder	3.28(1)	3.05(1)	3.13(1)	−		
Yom Kippur Observance	3.17(2)	2.97(2)	3.03(2)	−		
Sabbath Observance	2.89(3)	2.75(3)	2.87(3)			
Sitting *Shiva*—Mourning	2.82(4)	2.54(4)	2.57(5)	−	−	
Brit Milah—Circumcision	2.69(5)	2.33(7)	2.74(4)	−		+
Kosher Home	2.68(6)	2.34(6)	2.41(8)			
Kashrut—Dietary Laws	2.66(7)	2.38(5)	2.45(7)			
Sukkot	2.30(8)	2.08(9)	2.15(10)	−		
Expected Mitzvot	2.00(9)	2.17(8)	2.56(6)		+	+
Daily Worship	1.97(10)	1.99(10)	1.94(11)			
Mikvah—Family Purity	1.56(11)	1.56(11)	2.21(9)		+	+
Total, Knowledge of Major Rabbinic Practice Requirements*	26.97	25.59	27.07			
Total, Knowledge of Primary Jewish Blessings#	3.47	3.57	2.69	−	−	−

Jewish History and Issues

Shoah (Holocaust)	3.22(1)	3.05(1)	3.19(1)	−		+
Zionism	2.65(2)	2.34(2)	2.32(3)	−	−	
Biblical History	2.51(3)	2.34(3)	2.44(2)	−	−	
Postbiblical History	2.50(4)	2.29(4)	2.30(4)	−	−	−

Jewish Community Resources

The Sentinel	3.35(1)	2.47(4)	2.06(6)	−	−	
Jewish Community Centers	3.00(2)	2.80(1)	2.62(3)	−	−	
The Ark	2.82(3)	1.98(7)	2.17(5)	−	−	
Spertus College of Judaica	2.81(4)	2.78(2)	3.29(1)	+	+	+
Michael Reese Hospital	2.78(5)	2.69(3)	2.96(2)	−	−	
Jewish Vocational Service	2.74(6)	2.07(6)	1.76(9)	−	−	−
Mount Sinai Hospital	2.58(7)	2.42(5)	2.44(4)	−	−	
Council for Jewish Elderly	2.48(8)	1.97(8)	1.88(7)	−	−	
Board of Jewish Education	2.43(9)	1.85(9)	1.58(10)	−	−	
Jewish Family and Community Services	2.34(10)	1.81(10)	1.86(8)	−	−	
Jewish Children's Bureau	2.34(11)	1.60(11)	1.52(11)	−	−	
Hebrew Theological College	2.15(12)	1.54(12)	1.36(12)	−	−	
Drexel Home	2.09(13)	1.22(13)	0.87(13)	−	−	−
Response Center	1.26(14)	1.00(15)	0.72(15)	−	−	−
Associated Talmud Torahs	1.67(15)	1.11(14)	0.80(14)	−	−	−
Total, Knowledge of Major Jewish Agencies*	37.01	29.23	27.59			

* "−" indicates that the comparison score is significantly lower than the born Jews' score; in the case of PR vs. CV, partners represent born Jews.

* "+" indicates that the comparison score is significantly higher than the born Jews' score; in the case of PR vs. CV, partners represent born Jews.

** Variables are listed within each category from highest to lowest according to the in-married, born Jew mean; bracketed number (for example, (1)) is the rank.

A description of the Total (scale) variables can be obtained from Dr. Forster.

TABLE 4.8
COMPARISONS AMONG BORN JEWS' (BJ), PARTNERS' (PR), AND CONVERTS' (CV) PATTERNS OF REGULAR JEWISH RELIGIOUS PRACTICES

Judaism Variables**	Means			Significant Differences*		
	Born Jews	Partners	Converts	BJ vs. PR	BJ vs. CV	PR vs. CV
Religious Practices						
Have a Hanukah menorah*	0.99(1)	0.88(1)	0.91(1)	—		+
Belong to a Synagogue*	0.99(2)	0.64(14)	0.69(12)	—	—	
Participate in Passover Seder	3.89(3)	3.74(2)	3.52(2)	—	—	—
Attend Yom Kippur Services	3.77(4)	3.40(6)	3.39(5)	—	—	
Have a Jewish Prayer Book*	0.93(5)	0.82(10)	0.79(6)	—	—	—
Light Hanukah Candles	3.67(6)	3.65(5)	3.40(4)		—	—
Have a Jewish Bible*	0.92(7)	0.78(12)	0.75(9)	—	—	
Exchange Hanukah Presents	3.68(8)	3.23(8)	3.45(3)	—	—	
Attend Rosh Hashanah Services	3.71(9)	3.34(7)	3.30(7)			
Have a *Mezzuzah* on Outside Doorway(s)*	0.90(10)	0.63(13)	0.73(10)	—	—	—
Know *Shema* in Hebrew*	0.89(11)	0.93(3)	0.77(8)			
Know *Kiddush* (Over Wine) in Hebrew*	0.89(12)	0.92(4)	0.68(14)		—	—
Know *Hamotzi* (Over Bread) in Hebrew*	0.89(13)	0.90(9)	0.59(15)		—	—
Know Candle Blessing in Hebrew*	0.80(14)	0.80(11)	0.70(11)		—	—*
Eat Only Unleavened Food During Passover	2.85(15)	2.38(16)	2.44(16)		—	
Fast on Yom Kippur	2.78(16)	2.81(15)	2.82(13)			
Light Sabbath Candles	2.15(17)	1.77(18)	2.15(18)	—		+
Say *Kiddush* over Wine (or Partner)	1.87(18)	1.42(20)	0.63(20)	—	—	
Attend Purim Services	1.89(19)	1.33(21)	1.84(19)	—		+
Attend Sabbath Services	2.10(20)	1.92(17)	2.33(17)	—		+
Have a *Mezzuzah* On Inside Doorway(s)*	0.28(21)	0.32(19)	0.25(23)	—		
Have a Home Sabbath Service	1.56(22)	1.19(22)	1.61(21)	—		+
Observe Sukkot	1.60(23)	1.17(23)	1.59(22)	—		+

Keep Kosher at Home	1.02(24)	0.70(27)	0.94(27)	−		−
Have Separate Passover Dishes*	0.17(25)	0.14(24)	0.17(24)			
Have an Active Role in Jewish Worship Services	1.21(26)	0.85(26)	0.77(29)	−	−	−
Refrain from Work on the Sabbath	0.71(27)	0.50(29)	1.00(26)		+	+
Engage in Formal Study of Judaism	1.11(28)	0.99(25)	1.24(25)	+	+	+
Eat Kosher Away from Home	0.72(29)	0.52(28)	0.93(28)	+	−	+
Attend a Daily Minyan	0.34(30)	0.21(31)	0.18(32)			
Say Daily Morning Prayers	0.30(31)	0.20(32)	0.69(30)	−	−	+
Use *Tefillin* (or Partner)	0.25(32)	0.24(30)	0.24(31)	−		−
Total, Major Rabbinic Religious Practices##	25.41	23.35	23.81	−	−	
Total, Supportive Rabbinic Religious Practices##	6.44	5.43	5.25	−	−	−
Importance of Religious Activities						
Live Near a Synagogue	3.03(1)	1.46(6)	2.83(4)	−	−	+
Continued Study of Judaism	3.02(2)	2.87(2)	3.23(2)			+
Learn to Follow the Prayers	2.86(3)	2.85(3)	3.25(1)		+	+
Learn the Prayers in Hebrew	2.82(4)	2.72(4)	3.03(3)			+
Learn Hebrew	2.54(5)	2.36(5)	2.53(5)			
Bar or Bat Mitzvah	2.41(6)	2.93(1)	1.58(6)	+	−	−
Total, Importance of Major Rabbinic Religious Concerns##	15.75	14.52	14.61	−		

* "−" indicates that the comparison score is significantly lower than the born Jews' score; in the case of PR vs. CV, partners represent born Jews.

+ "+" indicates that the comparison score is significantly higher than the born Jews' score; in the case of PR vs. CV, partners represent born Jews.

** Variables are listed within each category from highest to lowest according to the in-married, born Jew mean; bracketed number (for example, (1)) is the rank.

Some variables permit only a yes or no response (for example, having or not having a Hanukah menorah); therefore, category means are shown by the rank order as based on a collapse of the positive categories on scale items to compare with "Yes, I do" responses.

Yes or no item.

A description of the Total (scale) variables can be obtained from Dr. Forster.

TABLE 4.9
COMPARISONS AMONG BORN JEWS' (BJ), PARTNERS' (PR), AND CONVERTS' (CV) REGULAR CHRISTIAN RELIGIOUS PRACTICES

Christian Variables**	Means			Significant Differences*		
	Born Jews	Partners	Converts	BJ vs. PR	BJ vs. CV	PR vs. CV
Decorate home at Christmas/Hanukah	2.03(1)	1.95(2)	2.45(3)		+	+
Send Christmas cards	1.53(2)	1.56(4)	1.85(4)		+	
Exchange Christmas presents with relatives	0.99(3)	2.22(1)	3.11(1)	+	+	+
Attend a Christmas family gathering	0.69(4)	1.89(3)	2.63(2)	+	+	+
Attend a Christian service	0.50(5)	0.47(7)	0.51(7)		+	
Exchange Christmas presents in own household	0.27(6)	1.00(5)	1.09(6)	+	+	

Attend Easter family gatherings	0.15(7)	0.92(6)	1.43(5)			+
Decorate a Christmas tree	0.07(8)	0.43(8)	0.49(8)	+	+	+
Attend a Christmas service	0.05(9)	0.30(9)	0.31(9)	+	+	+
Attend Easter services	0.04(10)	0.19(10)	0.22(10)	+	+	+
Total, Christian practices*	2.44	10.90	12.39	+	+	+

* "–" indicates that the comparison score is significantly lower than the born Jews' score; in the case of PR vs. CV, partners represent born Jews.

"+" indicates that the comparison score is significantly higher than the born Jews' score; in the case of PR vs. CV, partners represent born Jews.

** Variables are listed within each category from highest to lowest according to the in-married, born Jew mean; bracketed number (for example, (1)) is the rank.

* A description of the Total (scale) variables can be obtained from Dr. Forster.

TABLE 4.10

COMPARISONS AMONG BORN JEWS' (BJ), PARTNERS' (PR), AND CONVERTS' (CV) INVOLVEMENTS IN THE JEWISH COMMUNITY

	Means			Significant Differences*		
Ethnic Variables**	Born Jews	Partners	Converts	BJ vs. PR	BJ vs. CV	PR vs. CV
Jewish Ethnic Practice						
Have Jewish art on display*	0.87(1)	0.67(1)	0.79(1)	—	—	
Watch Jewish TV or films	2.86(2)	2.25(2)	2.77(2)	—	—	+
Subscribe to a Jewish newspaper*	0.65(3)	0.38(3)	0.54(3)	—	—	+
Belong to a Jewish organization*	0.60(4)	0.27(10)	0.38(6)	—	—	
Belong to a Synagogue-related group*	0.44(5)	0.16(12)	0.28(8)	—	—	
Read Jewishly related literature	2.21(6)	1.54(4)	2.15(4)	—	—	+
Attend Jewish groups	2.04(7)	0.98(9)	1.31(11)	—	—	+
Participate in ongoing Jewish education*	0.36(8)	0.16(11)	0.29(7)	—	—	
Wear Jewish jewelry	1.37(9)	1.41(5)	2.00(5)	—	+	+
Listen to Jewish music	1.83(10)	1.12(8)	1.28(12)	—	—	
Attend Jewish cultural events	1.88(12)	1.24(6)	1.65(10)	—	—	+
Serve as an officer for a Jewish organization	1.56(11)	0.55(14)	0.58(13)	—	—	
Attend Jewish lectures	1.70(13)	1.09(7)	1.65(9)	—	—	+
Belong to a YMHA or Jewish community center*	0.14(14)	0.11(13)	0.10(14)	—	—	
Teach or organize Jewish activities	1.07(15)	0.47(15)	0.52(15)	—	—	

Percent Jewish neighbors	2.14	2.27	2.54		—
Percent Jewish friends	75.00	54.50	45.74		
Percent give to Jewish charity	67.75	61.40	63.91	—	—
Total, Jewish ethnic inputs**	9.26	6.50	8.75	—	+
Importance of Ethnic Activities					
Support of Israel	3.58(1)	3.14(2)	2.78(3)	—	—
Visit to Israel	3.39(2)	3.03(3)	2.79(2)	—	—
Live near good public school	3.26(3)	3.39(1)	3.03(1)	—	—
Have a substantial number of Jewish neighbors	2.93(4)	2.64(4)	2.50(4)	—	
Aliyah to Israel for others	2.48(5)	2.35(5)	2.17(5)	—	
Aliyah to Israel for self	1.23(6)	1.84(6)	1.78(6)	+	+
Live near Jewish Day school	1.10(7)	1.45(7)	1.69(7)	+	+
Total, major rabbinic ethnic involvements**	13.54	12.99	12.00	—	

* "—" indicates that the comparison score is significantly lower than the born Jews' scores; in the case of PR vs. CV, partners represent born Jews.

"+" indicates that the comparison score is significantly higher than the born Jews' score; in the case of PR vs. CV, partners represent born Jews.

** Variables are listed within each category from highest to lowest according to the in-married, born Jew mean; bracketed number (for example, (1)) is the rank

Some variables permit only a yes or no response (for example, having or not having a Hanukah menorah); therefore, category means are shown by the rank order as based on a collapse of the positive categories on scale items to compare with "Yes, I do" responses.

Yes or no item.

A description of the Total (scale) variables can be obtained from Dr. Forster.

TABLE 4.11

COMPARISONS AMONG BORN JEWS' (BJ), PARTNERS' (PR), AND CONVERTS' (CV)
COMMITMENT TO JEWISH CHILD-REARING FOCUSES

| | Means | | | | Significant Differences* | | |
	Born Jews	Partners	Converts		BJ vs. PR	BJ vs. CV	PR vs. CV
*Child-Rearing Variables***							
General Religious Practices							
Believing in God	2.21(1)	2.27(1)	2.63(1)			+	+
Being Free to Choose Own Religion	1.41(2)	1.93(2)	2.26(2)			+	+
Jewish Religious Practices							
A Hebrew Name	2.80(1)	2.50(2)	2.29(4)		–	–	
A *Bar* or *Bat Mitzvah*	2.76(2)	2.49(3)	2.34(2)			–	
Circumcision or Dedication	2.74(3)	2.53(1)	2.43(1)			–	
A Jewish Part-Time Education	2.69(4)	2.34(4)	2.30(3)		–	–	
Believing that Jesus was not the Messiah	2.15(5)	1.72(5)	1.70(5)		–	–	
Confirmation	2.02(6)	1.48(6)	1.50(6)		–	–	
Not Participating in School Christmas or Easter Celebration	1.45(7)	1.12(8)	1.20(8)		–	–	
A Jewish Day School Education	1.15(8)	1.44(7)	1.34(7)		+	+	
Christian Practices							
Having Positive Beliefs About Jesus' Ministry	0.28(1)	0.55(1)	0.95(1)		+	+	+

Attending Christian Religious Services Being						
Baptized	0.18(2)	0.43(2)	0.37(2)	+	+	+
Being Baptized	0.06(3)	0.14(3)	0.28(3)	+	+	+
Total, Child Christian Practices*	4.40	5.43	5.88	+	+	+
Jewish Ethnic Involvements for Children						
Having a Strong Jewish Identity	2.89(1)	2.59(1)	2.30(1)	−	−	−
Raising a Jewish Family	2.85(2)	2.49(2)	2.18(2)	−	−	−
Marrying a Jew (or Convert)	2.72(3)	1.82(5)	1.36(5)	−	−	−
Having a Few Jewish Friends	2.46(4)	2.28(3)	2.10(3)	−	−	−
Visiting Israel	2.44(5)	1.99(4)	1.75(4)	−	−	−
Dating Only Jews	2.20(6)	1.12(9)	0.89(9)	−	−	−
Having Mostly Jewish Friends	2.13(7)	1.57(6)	1.31(6)	−	−	−
Attending a Jewish Summer Camp	1.58(8)	1.33(7)	1.30(7)	−	−	−
Study in Israel	1.43(9)	1.19(8)	1.05(8)	−	−	−
Aliyah to Israel	0.75(10)	0.95(10)	1.00(10)	−	+	+
Total, Child Major Jewish Involvements*	38.52	32.99	30.33	−	−	−

* "−" Indicates that the comparison score is significantly lower than the born Jews' score; in the case of PR vs. CV, partners represent born Jews.

"+" indicates that the comparison score is significantly higher than the born Jews' score; in the case of PR vs. CV, partners represent born Jews.

** Variables are listed within each category from highest to lowest according to the in-married, born Jew mean; bracketed number (for example, (1)) is the rank.

* A description of the Total (scale) variables can be obtained from Dr. Forster.

Bibliography

Angel, Marc D. "Another Halachic Approach to Conversion." *Tradition* (Winter-Spring 1972), 67–69.

Bamberger, Bernard J. *Proselytism in the Talmudic Period.* Cincinnati: Hebrew University College Press, 1939.

Bamberger, Bernard J. "Conversion to Judaism: Theologically Speaking." In David Max Eichhorn (ed.), *Conversion to Judaism: A History* (pp. 52–70). New York: Ktav, 1965.

Baron, Salo. *A Social and Religious History of the Jews* (Vol. 1). New York: Columbia University Press, 1952.

Berger, Graenum. "Intermarriage and the Failure of the American Jewish Community." *Proceedings of the Conference on Intermarriage and the Future of the American Jew.* New York: Commission on Synagogue Relations and Federation of Jewish Philanthropies of New York, December 1964.

Bernards, Rabbi Solomon (ed.). *Who Is A Jew? A Reader.* New York: Anti-Defamation League, 1972.

Bigman, Stanley K. *The Jewish Population of Greater Washington in 1956.* Portland: Jewish Community Council of Greater Washington, 1957.

Blatt, Serano. "Outreach." Letter to Rabbis, Temple Administrators, and Presidents. Spring 1986.

Braude, William G. *Jewish Proselytism in the First Five Centuries of the Common Era.* Providence, RI: Brown University Press, 1940.

Brodbar-Nemzer, Jay J. "Divorce and Group Commitment: The Case of the Jews." *Journal of Marriage and the Family* 48 (May 1986), 329–340.

Cardozo, Arlene Rossen. *Jewish Family Celebrations: The Sabbath, Festivals, and Ceremonies.* New York: St. Martin's, 1982.

Carmel, Abraham. "My Chosen People." *Tradition* 2 (Winter 1988), 15–27.

Cowan, Paul, and Cowan, Rachel. "Interfaith Couples: A Delicate Imbalance." *Hadassah* (October 1987), 22–25.

Cowan, Paul, and Cowan, Rachel. *Mixed Blessings: Marriage Between Jews and Christians*. New York: Doubleday, 1987.

Davis, Moshe. "Mixed Marriages in Western Jewry." *Jewish Journal of Sociology* (December 1968), 179–186.

Diamant, Anita. *The New Jewish Wedding*. New York: Summit, 1985.

Donin, Rabbi Hayim Halevy. *To Be A Jew: A Guide to Jewish Observance in Contemporary Life*. New York: Basic Books, 1972.

Dresner, Samuel H., and Sherwin, Bryon L. *Judaism: The Way of Sanctification*. New York: United Synagogue, 1978.

Edelheit, Joseph A. "Are We Ready for the New Jewish Community?" *Journal of Reform Judaism* (Winter 1957), 79–86.

Edelheit, Joseph A. *An Introduction to Judaism* (Course Outline). Chicago: Chicago Association of Reform Rabbis and Chicago Region Rabbinical Assembly, 1980.

Eichhorn, David Max (ed.). *Conversion to Judaism: A History and Analysis*. New York: Ktav, 1965.

Franzblau, Abraham N. "Conversion to Judaism: Psychologically Speaking." In *Conversion to Judaism: A History and Analysis* (pp. 189–202). New York: Ktav, 1965.

Friedman, Peter. "The Who, Whats, and Wheres of Jewish Chicago." *JUF News* (April 1986), 34–37.

Gallob, Ben. "Encourage Converts to Judaism in Interfaith Marriages, Urges Author." *Sentinel* (November 21, 1985), 20.

Gallob, Ben. "Cause of Conflict in Mixed Marriages Is Ethnic As Well As Religious-Based." *Sentinel* (March 6, 1986), 25.

Gallob, Ben. "Jews by Choice: Can They Meet the Expectations of Their Jewish Mate?" *Sentinel* (September 25, 1986), 21.

Gallob, Ben. "Jewish Conversion on Rise in U.S., Is No Longer a Topic to be Avoided." *Sentinel* (January 29, 1987), 26–27.

Gallob, Ben. "When One Spouse Chooses to Convert to Judaism. . . . in a Gentile Marriage." *Sentinel* (April 16, 1987), 47.

Gallob, Ben. "Intermarriage Reported to be Far More Likely Among Younger Jews." *Sentinel* (November 24, 1988), 27–29.

Gallob, Ben. "New Converts to Judaism Are Not Always White with European Roots." *Sentinel* (January 11, 1990), 22B.

Ginzberg, Louis. *The Legends of the Jews* (Vol. 4). New York: Jewish Publication Society, 1941.

Glazer, Nathan. "Jews and Intermarriage." *Sentinel* (June 25, 1987), 14.

Goldenberg, Naomi Ruth. "A Response to Anne Roiphe on the Jewish Family: The Problem of Intermarriage." *Tikkun* 2(1), 118–119.

Goldscheider, Calvin. "Social Change and Jewish Continuity." In Richard T. Schaefer and Robert P. Lamm (eds.), *Introducing Sociology: A Collection of Readings* (pp. 278–280). New York: McGraw-Hill, 1987.

Goldscheider, Calvin, and Zuckerman, Alan S. *The Transformation of the Jews*. Chicago: University of Chicago Press, 1984.

Goldstein, Sidney. "Population Trends in American Jewry." *Judaism* 36 (Spring 1987), 135–146.

Goldstein, Sidney, and Goldscheider, Calvin. *Jewish Americans: Three Generations in a Jewish Community*. Englewood Cliffs, NJ: Prentice-Hall, 1968.

Gordis, Robert. *Judaism in a Christian World*. New York: Free Press, 1966.

Gordon, Albert Isaac. *The Nature of Conversion*. Boston: Beacon Press, 1967.

Graetz, Heinrich. *History of the Jews*. Philadelphia: Jewish Publication Society, 1949.

Greenberg, Blu. *How to Run a Traditional Jewish Household*. New York: Simon & Schuster, 1983.

Gruzen, Lee F. *Raising Your Jewish/Christian Child*. New York: Dodd, Mead, 1987.

Harlow, Jules (ed. and trans.). *Siddur Sim Shalom*. New York: United Synagogue of America, 1985.

Harris, Monford. *On Entering Jewish Existence: Towards a Theology of Conversion*. Unpublished manuscript. Chicago: Spertus College of Judaica, 1970.

Hartman, David. *A Living Covenant: The Innovative Spirit in Traditional Judaism*. New York: Free Press, 1985.

Helfgott, Esther Altshol. "A Convert's View of Jewish Men and Women." *JUF News* (September 1987), 78.

Herberg, Will. *Judaism and Modern Man: An Interpretation of Jewish Religion*. New York: Atheneum, 1970.

Herman, Simon N. *Jewish Identity: A Social-Psychological Perspective*. Beverly Hills, CA: Sage, 1977.

Hertz, Joseph H. (ed.). *The Pentateuch and Haftorahs*. London: Soncino Press, 1938.

Hertzberg, Arthur. "Modern Judaism and the Emancipation: A Reassessment After 2 Centuries." *Modern Judaism* 1 (1946), 1–19.

Heschel, Abraham Joshua. *God in Search of Man: A Philosophy of Judaism*. New York: Farrar, Straus, & Giroux, 1955.

Hierich, H. "Change of Heart: A Test of Some Widely Held Theories about Religious Conversion." *American Journal of Sociology* 83 (1977), 653–679.

Hirsh, Rabbi Richard. "Confronting the 'December Dilemma': Intermarried Families and the Holidays." *Sentinel* (December 25, 1986), 29, 31.

Huberman, Stephen. "Conversion to Judaism: An Analysis of Family Matters." *Judaism* (Summer 1981), 312–321.

Huberman, Stephen. "From Christianity to Judaism: Religion Changes in American Society." *Conservative Judaism* 36 (Fall 1982), 20–28.

Jacobs, Louis. *A Jewish Theology*. New York: Behrman, 1983.

Jakobovits, Immanuel. "The Timely and Timeless." *Tradition* (Spring 1989), 164–215.

Kalb, Harold, and Weinshanker, Jack. "Conservative Movement Milestone: Joint Conference Intermarriage and Conversion." *United Synagogue Review* (Fall 1987), 6, 24.

Kaplan, Mordecai. *Judiasm as a Civilization*. New York: Macmillan, 1957. (Original work published in 1934.)

Katz, Jacob. *Exclusiveness and Tolerance*. London: Oxford University Press, 1961.

Kaufmann, Yehezkel. *The Religion of Israel* (trans. and abridged by Moshe Greenberg). Chicago: University of Chicago Press, 1960.

Kertzer, Rabbi Morris N. *What Is A Jew?* (4th ed.). New York: Collier, 1978.

Kukoff, Lydia. *Choosing Judaism*. New York: Union of American Hebrew Congregations, 1981.

Lerner, Rabbi Stephen C. "Jews by Choice." *Rabbinical Assembly Proceedings* 45 (1983), 71–76.

Levenson, Alan. "Reform Attitudes, in the Past, Toward Intermarriage." *Judaism* 38 (Summer 1989), 320–332.

Levin, Michael Graubart. *Journey to Tradition: Odyssey of a Born-Again Jew*. New York: Ktav, 1986.

Lieberman, S. Zevulun. "Syrian Jews." *Tradition* 23 (Spring 1988), 27–52.

Linzer, Norman. *The Jewish Family: Authority and Tradition in Modern Perspective.* New York: Human Sciences Press, 1984.

Mayer, Egon. "A Cure for Intermarriage?" *Moneit* 4, 6 (June 1979), 62–64.

Mayer, Egon. *Children of Intermarriage: A Study in Patterns of Identification and Family Life.* New York: American Jewish Committee, 1983.

Mayer, Egon. "Jews by Choice: Their Impact on the Contemporary American Jewish Community." *Rabbinical Assembly Proceedings* 45 (1983), 57–70.

Mayer, Egon. *Achieving Identity in an Ascriptive Community: The Dilemma of Conversion in Modern Judaism.* Unpublished manuscript. New York: Brooklyn College, 1984.

Mayer, Egon. *Love and Tradition: Marriage Between Jews and Christians.* New York: Plenum, 1985.

Mayer, Egon. "From Outrage to Outreach: Alternative Jewish Responses to Intermarriage." *Outlook* (Fall 1987), 12–13.

Mayer, Egon, and Augar, Amy. *Conversion Among the Intermarried: Choosing to Become Jewish.* New York: American Jewish Committee, 1987.

Mayer, Egon, and Sheingold, Carl. *Intermarriages and the Jewish Future: A National Study in Summary.* New York: American Jewish Committee, 1979.

Minkin, Jacob S. *The Shaping of the Modern Mind.* New York: Thomas Yoselott Press, 1963.

Moore, George Foote. *Judaism in the First Centuries of the Christian Era: The Age of the Tannaim.* Cambridge, MA: Harvard University Press, 1927.

Netter, Perry. "Will Your God Really Be My God?" *Moment* (January/February 1989), 44–47.

Petsonk, Judy, and Rensen, Jim. *The Intermarriage Handbook: A Guide for Jews and Christians.* New York: Arbor, 1988.

Petuchowski, Jacob J. "Realism About Mixed Marriages." *CCAR Journal* (October 1966), 35–40.

"Proselytes." *Encyclopedia Judaica* (pp. 1182–1194). New York: MacMillian, 1972.

Rabbi's Manual. New York: Rabbinical Assembly of America, 1965.

Rosenman, Yehuda. "The Jewish Family: Lights and Shadows." *Judaism* 36 (Spring 1987), 147–153.

Rosenthal, Erich. "Studies of Jewish Intermarriage in the U.S." In Morris Fine and Milton Himmelfarb (eds.), *American Jewish*

Yearbook, 1963 (pp. 3–71) New York: American Jewish Committee, 1963.

Rozwaski, Chaim Z. "Jewish Law and Intermarriage." *Jewish Life* (July/August 1969), 18–23.

Rubenstein, Richard L. "Intermarriage and Conversion on the American College Campus." In Werener J. Cahnman (ed.), *Intermarriage and Jewish Life*. New York: Shocken, 1963.

Sandberg, Neil C. *Jewish Life in Los Angeles: A Window to Tomorrow*. New York: Lanhainm, 1986.

Schechter, Solomon. *Aspects of Rabbinic Theology*. New York: Shocken, 1981. (Original work published in 1909.)

Schneider, Susan Weidman. "Review: Love and Tradition: Marriage Between Jews and Christians." *United Synagogue Review* (Spring 1987), 32.

Schwartz, Arnold. "Intermarriage in the U.S." In Morris Fine, Milton Himmelfarb, and Martha Jelenko (eds.), *American Jewish Yearbook 1970* (pp. 101–121). New York: American Jewish Committee, 1970.

Sherwin, Byron. *Mystical Theology and Social Dissent: The Life and Works of Judah Lowe of Prague*. Rutherford, NJ: Fairleigh-Dickenson University Press, 1982.

Silberman, Charles. *A Certain People: American Jews and Their Lives Today*. New York: Simon & Schuster, 1985.

Silverstein, Rabbi Alan. "Project Joseph: Responding to Intermarriage." *Outlook* (Fall 1987), 14–15.

Sklare, Marshall. "Intermarriage and Jewish Survival." *Commentary* 49, 3 (March 1970), 51–58.

Sklare, Marshall. *America's Jews*. New York: Random House, 1971.

Sklare, Marshall, and Greenblum, Joseph. *Jewish Identity on the Suburban Frontier* (2nd ed.). Chicago: University of Chicago Press, 1979.

Soloveichik, Joseph B. "Beyn Brisk L'Boston" [Between Brisk and Boston]. *Hadoar* (September 5, 1986), 5–9.

Stern, Malcolm H. "Jewish Marriage and Intermarriage in the Federal Period (1776–1840)." *American Jewish Archives* 19 (November 1967), 142–143.

Strassfeld, Michael. *The Jewish Holidays: A Guide and Commentary*. New York: Harper and Row, 1985.

Straus, Roger A. "Religious Conversion as a Personal and Collective Accomplishment." *Sociological Analysis* 40, 2 (1979), 158–165.

Tobin, Gary. "Understanding and Dealing with the Reasons for Intermarriage." *JUF News* (July 1990), 48, 63.

Ullman, Chana. "Cognitive and Emotional Antecedents of Religious Conversions." *Journal of Personality and Social Behavior* 43, 1 (1982), 183–192.

Waxman, Chaim I. *America's Jews in Transition.* Philadelphia: Temple University Press, 1983.

Waxman, Ruth B. (ed.). "How the Emancipation and the Enlightenment Changed Jewish History." *Judaism* 38, 44 (Fall 1989).

Winkler, Gershon. "Intermarriage: What If It's Too Late?" *Jewish Homemaker* (April–May, 1986), 5–7.

Yearbook, Conference of American Rabbis, XIX. New York: Central Conference of American Rabbis, 1909.